# Yorkshire
# Terriers

*Edited by the Staff of T.F.H. Publications*

Poster **A.** A photographic masterpiece by Missy Yuhl showing Champion Dot's Top Banana, owned by Dorothy Gaunt.

Poster **B.** The multi-titled International Champion Estugo's Stargazer at sixteen months of age. Photographed by Johnell Kinsey for owners Hugo J. Ibanez and Stephen B. Maggard.

Poster **C.** Perhaps they aren't of championship caliber, but you'll seldom find a more attentive trio.

Distributed in the UNITED STATES by T.F.H. Publications, Inc., 211 West Sylvania Avenue, Neptune City, NJ 07753; in CANADA by H & L Pet Supplies Inc., 27 Kingston Crescent, Kitchener, Ontario N2B 2T6; Rolf C. Hagen Ltd., 3225 Sartelon Street, Montreal 382 Quebec; in ENGLAND by T.F.H. Publications Limited, 4 Kier Park, Ascot, Berkshire SL5 7DS; in AUSTRALIA AND THE SOUTH PACIFIC by T.F.H. (Australia) Pty. Ltd., Box 149, Brookvale 2100 N.S.W., Australia; in NEW ZEALAND by Ross Haines & Son, Ltd., 18 Monmouth Street, Grey Lynn, Auckland 2 New Zealand; in SINGAPORE AND MALAYSIA by MPH Distributors (S) Pte., Ltd., 601 Sims Drive, # 03/07/21, Singapore 1438; in the PHILIPPINES by Bio-Research, 5 Lippay Street, San Lorenzo Village, Makati Rizal; in SOUTH AFRICA by Multipet Pty. Ltd., 30 Turners Avenue, Durban 4001. Published by T.F.H. Publications Inc., Ltd. the British Crown Colony of Hong Kong.

# Contents

Cover photo by Robert Pearcy.

Back cover: *Upper left:* Ch. Cupoluv's Fair
LeGrand, top-producing stud dog owned by
Zinaida Daricek of Avondale, Pennsylvania.
*Upper right:* Silverwinds Spirit of Apollo
with Ch. Wildweir Candytuft, owned by
Elissa Taddie of West Chester, Pennsylvania.
*Bottom:* C. N. Shook's (Cedar Wood Studio)
photo of, left to right, Ch. Gayelyn Gilded
Lilly, Ch. Windsor Gayelyn Gilded Lilly,
Ch. Ozmilion Playboy.

# Introduction

The proper introduction to a book like this one is a list of other good books about dogs, because no relatively small book could hope to cover comprehensively all of the specialized topics that a serious dog fancier can become involved with. Breeding, training, exhibiting, health care—they're all important topics, each one deserving a big volume of its own for proper exposition. The following books are all published by T.F.H. Publications and are recommended to you for additional information.

*Dog Behavior, Why Dogs Do What They Do* by Dr. Ian Dunbar (H-1016) is a thorough and enlightening exploration of all aspects of canine behavior and the relationship between man and dog. The author, a noted specialist in the field of animal behavior, discusses canine communication, social and sexual behaviors, and the physical and sensory capacities and capabilities of dogs, among other topics.

*Dog Training* by Lew Burke (H-962) reveals the secrets behind the methods successfully used by the author, a premier trainer of dogs for individuals, industry, and the government. Lew Burke concentrates on understanding dogs' needs in relation to the needs of their owner, and he uses dogs' psychological makeup to keep dogs happy by being obedient.

*Successful Dog Show Exhibiting* by Anna Katherine Nicholas (H-993) is an excellent how-to manual for purebred dog owners who are thinking about entering the world of dog show competition. The book includes detailed explanations of dog show classes, step-by-step descriptions of the judging process (including what the judge looks for), ring behavior do's and don'ts for both dog and handler, and advantages and disadvantages of professional handlers versus showing your own dog. The author, a judge who's been part of the world of dogs for over 50 years, knows her subject well and makes it understandable for the reader.

*Dog Breeding* by Ernest H. Hart (H-958) is an easy-to-read account of all the things a person needs to know about mating dogs to upgrade the breed. The mechanics, techniques, and

# *Introduction*

results of breeding, the physiology of the bitch and stud dog, gestation, whelping, fertility, how to build a strain, and how genetics can actually be used by the breeder are among the subjects covered in detail by the author.

*Dog Breeding for Professionals* by Dr. Herbert Richards (H-969) is a straightforward discussion of how to breed dogs of various sizes and how to care for newborn puppies. The many aspects of breeding (including possible problems and practical solutions) are covered in great detail. The explicit photos of canine sexual activities may offend some readers.

*Dog Owner's Encyclopedia of Veterinary Medicine* by Allan H. Hart, B.V.Sc. (H-934) is a comprehensive treatise on canine disease and disorders. It is written on the premise that dog owners should recognize the symptoms and understand the treatments of most diseases of dogs, so that dog owners can properly communicate with their veterinarian or give treatment to their dogs. Proper nutrition, parasite problems, and first-aid measures are also described.

• • • •

In addition to the foregoing, the following individual breed books of interest to readers of this book are available at pet shops and book stores.

*The Book of the Yorkshire Terrier*
*By Joan McDonald Brearley*
ISBN 0-87666-940-2
**TFH H-1066**
Though descended from a rugged European environment, this hardy toy breed requires special maintenance and grooming care, and *The Book of the Yorkshire Terrier* provides readers with all this practical advice and much, much more. In addition to the valuable information about grooming, breeding, showing, training, and routine maintenance, the book provides a wealth of fascinating text dealing with the history of the breed and its developers—all highlighted with enchanting photos (including many full-color photos).
*Hard cover, 8½ x 11"; 352 pages*
*87 full-color photos, more than 400 black and white photos*

# History and Origins of the Dog

Where there are people there are dogs. Whether they are stray dogs roaming the alleys of an eastern town, sheepdogs in mountain pastures, or purebred toy dogs living luxuriously in a modern western city, dogs undoubtedly like to be near people.

People like dogs too. They like them for all sorts of reasons—because they do a good job for them, guarding their homes and property, herding their livestock, keeping down vermin, or hunting and retrieving game. People like a dog because he's fun to be with, a good companion to share a game, a walk, or a warm fire, and a friendly creature who thinks his human master is just great.

The bond between man and dog is a unique relationship. There is no other quite the same between man and other domesticated animals. Man keeps sheep and cattle, ducks and chickens because they are useful in providing food, but the deep friendship, the reliance on one another, is not there. The horse perhaps builds up some relationship with his human master, but with rare exceptions it isn't real friendship—mostly it is based on trainability through physical contact with man, and on the reward of sugar and oats. Horses are basically still wild animals at heart—they don't particularly want a human friend.

Cats come and go in the human home; sometimes they get very fond of their human friends, but however long the cat lives with people, it retains its independence. Its devotion is based mainly on an appreciation of the food and warmth that it gets from man. If they go, so does the cat. It too remains basically a wild animal, but one intelligent enough to appreciate that food and shelter can come the easy way. Nevertheless, if it has to, it is perfectly capable of leading an independent existence.

Children keep hamsters, rabbits, pigeons, rats and mice and even insects as pets—but the devotion is usually more on the human side than the animals'.

With dogs, it's different. The affection between man and dog is mutual. We love 'em as much as they love us.

Yet for all this close companionship, this mutual devotion which has existed for such an incredibly long time, we know very little about the history and origins of the dog. To give him a scientific label, the dog is a member of the genus *Canis*.

We know, from fossils mostly, that the dog's immediate ancestors probably existed about half a million years ago.

## Early Origins

Nobody really knows for sure, but it is thought that the history of the dog began, in a remote sort of way, as long ago as 40 million years. There was a small family of carnivores (meat-eaters) then called *Miacidae*.

The *Miacidae* family had two descendants, one called *Daphaenus,* which eventually gave rise to the bears. The other was called *Cynodictis,* and was a smaller creature. From this creature there eventually evolved a dog-like animal called *Tomarctus,* which is thought to be the ancestor of dogs, wolves and jackals.

In the past it was often believed that the wolf and the jackal were the ancestors of the dog. All three are scientifically classified as being in the *Canis* family, but it has now been accepted by some authorities, that, though they are related, they are all separate offshoots of

*Tomarctus.* Other authorities hold that our dogs are descendants of the wolf.

Of course it is a long way from *Tomarctus,* the granddaddy of them all, to the modern dog that we know. *Tomarctus* had descendants. They developed differently in different places. Thousands of years went by, and sometime during this period man-like creatures met dog-like creatures.

All of this is unrecorded, and the sparse information available is based mostly on the evidence of geologists and archeologists working from fossilized remains.

They can give an approximate date for a type of prehistoric dog living domestically. It is placed between 6000 and 3000 B.C. A portion of the remains of a dog of no specific breed were found buried next to the remains of a woman on the coast of Zeeland.

There have also been archeological discoveries of domesticated dogs in Switzerland and in several other places, all prehistoric.

From this authorities conclude that dogs must have been domesticated in other parts of the world during those periods. As evolution takes such a long time, it is reasonable to suppose dogs must

# History and Origins of the Dog

have been living in some kind of association with man many thousands of years before that.

They say that domestication could have taken place any time from 50,000 to 250,000 years ago. This would make the dog a very old friend indeed.

## Man and Dog Meet

How did man and dog become associated in the first place? Since we've agreed it must have happened long before the time of recorded history, we can only guess. Both primitive man and primitive dog were hunters. Their paths must have crossed sometime or another. Perhaps man on one of his hunting expeditions caught a dog and used it for food—and kept on hunting it.

Maybe primitive man came across a female dog with puppies at some time, took them home to his cave or hole and kept them because he found that they could be fattened up for better eating. Perhaps playing outside the cave one day, Junior primitive man's son and heir, and his baby sisters found that the puppies romped and played rather attractively, and primitive man and his wife watched indulgently.

Somehow, somewhere, perhaps in several places in the world around about the same time, primitive man discovered that the dog was more than just another wild animal to be hunted, killed and eaten.

He discovered that instead of being a rival on the hunt for food, the dog would go along and help. He discovered that the dog would make a noise, give warning when danger approached. He discovered that the young of dogs were attractive play companions for his own young, that if the puppies grew up in the human encampment they became friendly and affectionate.

The dog too probably discovered that food was easier to come by in the vicinity of humans. The odd bone that primitive man threw over his shoulder when he'd finished with it probably gave primitive dog hours of pleasure chewing. Perhaps a chance incident like that was the first step ever in animal training—the first time mankind discovered that there were ways other than killing to bring an animal under control.

Why the dog should be willing to stay near man instead of running away as all other animals would do is one of the freaks of nature. It is a freak that has paid good dividends to both.

# History and Origins of the Dog

## How Different Breeds Originated

We've already said that either *Tomarctus,* the dog-like animal, or the wolf was probably the ancestor of the true dog, which is known scientifically as *Canis familiaris. Canis familiaris* developed into various forms.

The earliest date that can be put to a specific type is about 4000 B.C., which is the date given to the remains of *Canis familiaris palustris* which were found around the Swiss Lakes. Any of the various types of *Canis familiaris* could be earlier or later. Nobody knows for certain. Perhaps in the future more archeological searches will turn up new evidence that will tell us more. Otherwise, the farthest back we can go is to the beginning of recorded history, which is 4000 to 3000 B.C. There is evidence that a greyhound type of dog like the Saluki, and a Mastiff type were in existence then. There are representations of them both on an ancient green slate tablet which was found at Thebes and dates back to 4000 B.C.

On some tombs of ancient Egypt, dating back to 2200 to 2000 B.C., there are depicted hunting hounds of the Saluki type, as well as a heavier, mastiff-like dog, and a hunting dog with prick ears and a tightly curled tail not unlike a bigger, longer bodied Basenji. These tombs also show some dogs shorter in the legs and with thicker coats.

There is a dark-coated one with a tassled tail, and another with a spotted pattern marking and a curled tail.

## The Effects of Nature

All dogs started off as hunters, but they would hunt different kinds of prey, depending on where they lived. Where the natural animals of the area were fast moving creatures, then the dogs would have to develop the kind of body that would move even faster—like the lean sight-hunting breeds of the greyhound type who can spot a moving object a long way away and chase it at terrific speed.

Where the natural animals lived in dense cover, in forests, with plenty of undergrowth, then the hunting dog would need to have a good tracking nose to seek out his food. Where the prey lived in burrows underground, the dog after his dinner would need to have not only a good nose but the instinct to dig

# History and Origins of the Dog

down into the ground. Dogs hunting big animals would need to be bigger and fiercer to combat their adversaries.

Climate too would make a difference. Dogs living in the cold parts of Northern Europe and North America would need thick, dense coats to survive the icy conditions. Dogs that lived in thick forests and jungles would need to be smooth coated because a long coat would tangle in the undergrowth. Dogs in hot climates would develp short coats for coolness.

Man and dog teamed up, as we have seen, and man found that the dog could be useful. Eventually he would discover that the different kinds of dog could do different jobs. So man started to dabble in the development of the dog. He kept some kinds of dogs for hunting, some for guarding his property.

As man grew more civilized and started to keep animals around his encampment to raise for food instead of having to go out and hunt for meat all the time, he discovered that dogs could be used to guard his livestock, and then to herd them for him.

Gradually, under man's guidance, physical qualities and qualities of temperament and character began to be developed and fixed.

## The Appearance of Breeds

Most of the early dogs had a natural length of nose and width of head. Quite early in the history of dogs, however, another kind of dog appeared. This is the dwarf. This does not mean a miniature. The proportions of any miniature are exactly like the bigger version; only the size varies. A true dwarf, however, is quite different. The limbs and body are foreshortened and malformed, giving an abnormal appearance. How these dwarfs first appeared is not known. It was probably by what is called mutation. Mutations are one of the mysteries of nature—they just happen. Very little about how and why they happen naturally is known.

Enough of these dwarfs survived, and produced their own kind, to influence the varieties of dogs. How long it took we do not know, but there are signs of dwarfed ancestry in any breed which has crooked front legs, loosened folds of skin, squashed-up face, and very broad, domed skulls.

Man has of course encouraged some of these features, mostly perhaps because they appealed to him. Man has mixed them up and introduced them into other breeds. As a result you have such varying

# History and Origins of the Dog

kinds of dog as the Bloodhound, the Boxer, the Bulldog, the Basset Hound, the Welsh Corgi, the Pug, the Pekingese, the Japanese Spaniel, and many more, all of which show some signs of having "dwarf" characteristics, perhaps introduced a long, long way back in their ancestry. Small dogs like the Pekingese are the most obvious examples of an almost complete dwarf dog, deliberately bred that way by man.

Dogs like the Chihuahua and the Miniature Pinscher and the Toy Poodle are not dwarfs. They are midgets—miniatures—exact replicas of their bigger relatives. Small specimens occur in any living thing, including people. In dogs, man has deliberately encouraged the miniature and "bred down" to it.

As man continued to develop his civilization, he continued to create new breeds of dogs to suit his various needs. Man also moved about the world more easily, and dogs moved with him so that dogs from different kinds of places were interbred. Some kinds of dogs became extinct; new kinds were created. Some kinds of dogs remained basically the same for thousands of years.

It is thought that there are at present between 400 and 500 distinct breeds of dog in the world. In another hundred years there might be more or less. Many of them are man-made. The dog has come a long way from old *Cynodictis*. He probably still has a long way to go. In all that changing, one thing has remained unchanged, and that is the strength of the dog's unique relationship with man.

## The Dog at Work

We've seen that the earliest work the dog did, some thousands of years ago, was to work alongside primitive man, first in hunting, then as watchdog, guard of his master's property, home and livestock, and later in herding his livestock.

Very early in their history dogs were also a form of food and in some parts of the world they were raised, and still are raised, to provide meat.

Throughout the centuries, the dog's usefulness to man has extended, until today it reaches very sophisticated and advanced forms.

Hunting dogs can be classed among the oldest. In ancient Babylonia, and in the Egypt of the Pharaohs, they were highly valued for this. They include the "sighthounds"—fast greyhound types; the

# History and Origins of the Dog

"scent-hounds"—heavier and slower, and usually hunted in packs or groups. Getting nearer to modern times the short-legged terriers and small breeds like the Dachshund, which go to earth and drive the prey above ground for the scent-hounds to kill; and finally the sporting dogs, the pointers and setters, the retrievers and spaniels, all of whom assist man by finding and retrieving, while their master does the actual killing with his gun.

The guarding dogs are almost as old as the hunters. They defend their master and his property. Mostly they are big breeds, starting with the Molussus of olden times, developing into the Mastiff, the sheep-guarding kinds like the Komondor, and the heavy coated dogs of the Greek mountains.

Guard dogs generally, though, are not uncontrollable, vicious animals. To make the best use of them mankind had to temper their fierceness and power with intelligence. Powerful guard dogs have always had the reputation of never attacking on sight, but only when the intruder interferes with their master's property, their master's person, or attacks the dog himself. The culmination of man's efforts in breeding this kind of dog is seen in the modern guard dog,

the wonderfully trainable German Shepherd Dog, and the supremely efficient Doberman Pinscher.

In early times, the massive guard breeds were used in actual battle. Big and fierce, they were made even more ferocious looking with spiked collars, and they were protected by special suits of armor. Dogs were used for fighting as late as the 16th and 17th centuries.

The modern war dog is a different type—his value lies not just in his size and fierceness but primarily in his intelligence. Dogs have been trained for sentry duty, for scout work, for messenger duty, for patrol work, and as sled and pack dogs. With their marvelous olfactory abilities they were particularly successful in things like mine detection!

Modern war dogs don't need to be as massive as their ancient Mastiff predecessors. Mostly they have been German Shepherds, Doberman Pinschers, Giant Schnauzers, Airedales, farm Collies, and even Dalmatians.

At home, the shepherding and droving dogs did, and still do, provide wonderful service to their masters. There are the Collies, of various kinds, the cattle dogs like the Australian Kelpies, and the little Welsh Corgi among others.

# History and Origins of the Dog

## Legends of the Dog

Because of the dog's special relationship to mankind from early times, it is inevitable that many stories should grow up around this. Man is an inveterate gossip, and he loves a good story. Actions and behavior on the part of his canine companion intrigue, delight or puzzle him. He likes to tell his neighbor, sometimes with pride, sometimes with wonder.

Many legends are told of how dog and man first became firm friends. One tells how God made Adam and Eve, but during the night they were eaten by a serpent. So He made them again, but again they were eaten by a serpent. God was extremely angry, so He made Adam and Eve again, and also made a dog to protect them. When the serpent came in the night, the dog ferociously drove the serpent away.

Another story is very ancient. God created the world and everything in it. Man He made last of all, and He was very pleased with this creation. but man was very bad, and God got very angry with him, so angry that He caused a great rift to open in the earth cutting off man from all other animals. But the dog was so devoted to man that it leaped over the widening gap to join man. And the dog has been man's faithful friend and companion ever since.

The fidelity of dogs is honored in many tales. From the ancient world comes the tale of Ulysses' dog, Argus. When Ulysses went off to travel the world, Argus was left behind. Ulysses did not return for ten years, and when he did he came disguised as a beggar. Only one friend recognized him instantly—his old dog Argus. Argus was old and very weak, and almost dying, but managed to crawl toward his long-lost master. Trying to lick his hand, he died.

In the war in 1860 between China and the Western Powers, when the French and British marched on Peking and sacked the Summer Palace of the Imperial family, five small "lion dogs" were found guarding the body of the Emperor's aunt, who had committed suicide. Such fidelity to their mistress obviously attracted the foreign invaders and perhaps their ferocity too—for the little dogs looted from the Palace were the first members of the breed that we now know as the Pekingese.

# History

The Yorkshire Terrier is one of the best-loved breeds of both the American and British dog-fancying public. His intelligence and courage are out of all proportion to his size. His good manners seem inherent, and actions match his charming elfin appearance. It's hard to imagine a more desirable pet. A wonderful friend and companion, he is also one of the most respected and sought-after of all dogs.

The proud owner of a Yorkshire Terrier has selected a pet that combines the sturdiness of terriers and the graciousness of toy breeds! The diminutive Yorkie—small of size but large of character—has a surprisingly independent personality. He can amuse himself and makes few demands on his owner apart from grooming.

It is difficult to imagine a more desirable pet: he is a wonderful household companion and, at the same time, one of the most respected and sought-after of show breeds. Over one hundred years old, the Yorkshire Terrier is definitely a "man-made" breed. Yet the real source of its beginning is still in doubt. In Yorkshire, England, where the breed was first developed, the residents kept many terriers and toy dogs as companions, and, undoubtedly, many crosses were made among them. This same district also produced the Airedale, the largest of all terriers, and some authorities hold that the two breeds came from common parentage.

## Development

The original Yorkshire was by no means a toy. His weight ran from 12 to 14 pounds. The size has been reduced through selective breeding. Unlike other breeds which were developed by men of leisure, the Yorkshire Terrier was the dog of the common man.

Some of the dwarfing of the Yorkie's size was accomplished within 20 years of the time the dog first became recognized as a breed. For some time the breed did not run true to type as far as weight was concerned, and specimens ranged from 2¾ to 13 pounds in the show ring! Even as late as 1880, when the Yorkie was introduced to American breeders, weights of the dogs were highly variable and unpredictable.

Most authorities agree that the development of the petite Yorkshire Terrier can be traced to the continued mating of two related breeds. The Paisley Terrier played a large part in the Yorkie's make-up. This extinct breed resembled the

# History

Skye Terrier in many respects, but the Paisley was shorter in the back. The Broken-Coated Scottish Terrier was also instrumental in the Yorkie's development. The mixture of the black-and-tan and white coat of this breed may account for the white hairs sometimes found on the chest and paws of newborn Yorkshire puppies.

The first dogs to be prominently mentioned in connection with the Yorkshire Terrier's origin were Swift's Old Crab and Kershaw's Old Kitty. The former was a Black-and-Tan Terrier from Manchester, and the latter was a blue terrier of the drop-ear Skye type. Huddersfield Ben, the first pillar of the Yorkshire breed, was the result of the mating of Old Crab and Old Kitty in 1850. A very potent sire, Huddersfield Ben transmitted his good qualities to his numerous progeny in a great degree, and he is largely responsible for the appearance of the modern Yorkshire Terrier.

These little dogs were not always known as Yorkshire Terriers. They were first shown in England under the classification of "Broken-Coated Scottish or Yorkshire Terriers." About 1870, Mozart, a son of Huddersfield Ben, won a first prize in the Variety Class at the Westmorland show and a reporter commented that "they ought no longer to be called Scottish Terriers but Yorkshire Terriers." The name was an immediate success; it subsequently caught on and was adopted.

Even the Yorkie's coat has undergone an evolution. Writing in 1857, in the third edition of *Dogs of the British Isles,* Stonehedge said: "Since the first edition of this book was published, a considerable change has taken place in the type of several of the terrier family. At that time, the Yorkshire Terrier was represented by an animal only slightly differing from the old Scottish dog; his shape being nearly or exactly the same, and his coat differing simply in being more silky. Such an animal was Bounce (a champion of that day), and by comparing his portrait with that of Huddersfield Ben, it will readily be seen that a great development of coat has been accomplished in the latter."

## Notable Yorkies

It has become a matter of pride for breeders to advance well-researched theories of the dog's background; and no matter how hot the debate may wax, all agree that since emerging as a recognized breed, the Yorkshire Terrier has been notable for courage, loyalty, and steadfastness. Greyfriars Bobby, who lived in Great Britain during the late 1800's, is a good example. Bobby was of the same root stock as our Yorkie and they share a common ancestry.

No history of the Yorkshire Terrier would be complete without including the story of Smokey, a purebred Yorkie who was found in a shell hole after an American charge into Japanese lines in the New Guinea jungle. Smokey became the dog of soldier William Wynne and went through 150 air raids, flew 12 air-sea rescue missions, and weathered a typhoon at Okinawa. Wynne, who had no previous experience in training dogs, taught her how to waltz, walk a tightrope, and jump through hoops. At Lingayen, the Signal Corps had to lay a telegraph wire through a 9-inch pipe under an airstrip. Smokey crawled 70 feet through the pipe, dragging a tow line attached to the wire. In her special parachute, Smokey learned how to make jumps from a 30-foot tower; and she also ate C-rations and Spam, took soldiers' vitamin pills, and was bathed in Wynne's helmet.

**Captions for color photos on pages 17 through 24:**
*Page 17: Photographer Robert Pearcy has caught the Yorkie's natural enthusiasm with his lens. Page 18: Sharo's Blue Magic Girl is the pride and joy of owner Charlene B. Roland. Page 19: Champion Amberlyn's Patent Pending, photographed by Missy Yuhl for owner Lynne Layman Kassidy. Page 20: Canadian Champion Myork Muffin's Magic, owned by Mr. and Mrs. Monroe Hall, has twice appeared on the cover of Yorkie Tales magazine. Page 21: Champion Dot's Call Me Melanie being awarded a show win by judge Irene Phillips Schlintz. Page 22: Although small in size, a Yorkie puppy has boundless energy. Page 23: With hair in braids is Chelsea Nimar Miss Money Penny, owned by Nina McIntire. Page 24: Champion Sun Sprite Gemstone, co-owned by Sun Sprite and Kesar Kennels, as photographed by the Lloyd W. Olson Studio.*

**Captions for color photos on pages 57 through 64:**
*Page 57: A Yorkie with one ear up and the other down as Robert Pearcy snapped the picture. Page 58: Having fun in the fields outside with Nikko Kennels in Escondido, California. Page 59: Everblue's Mint Julep, photographed by Jim Easterday for owner Arlene Mack. Page 60: The youthful Windfall's Carousel, owned by Gloria Knight-Bloch. Page 61: Shown at only twelve weeks of age is Jacolyn Kibets Honey Bear, owned by Shelby Stevens and Carolyn Servis. Page 62: Champion Gaytonglen's Fun N Frolic scoring points under judge Merrill Cohen for owner Gloria Bloch. Page 63: An adult and a pup, photographed together by Bernard W. Kernan. Page 64: Bright-eyed youth captured by Robert Pearcy.*

# Looks and Personality

Of all the toy breeds, there is no finer pet than the Yorkshire Terrier! He is small and sturdy, very lovable and absolutely fearless.

The Yorkshire Terrier differs from other toy breeds in one important and very enviable quality: his extraordinarily fine temperament. He is calm and even-tempered and has a sunny disposition at all times. Never nervous or finicky, the Yorkie is one of the most amiable and contented, yet active, dogs known! He is not a one-man dog but shows his affection to all in equal and generous measure—an ideal trait in any household pet but especially welcome when there are small children in evidence.

Perhaps the frosting on the cake is that the perfectly groomed Yorkie show dog is one of the most beautiful sights that a dog fancier can meet. The best known characteristic of this handsome breed is a long, silky, and perfectly straight coat. In color, the Yorkshire Terrier is a beautiful steel blue from the tip of his head to the root of his tail, a rich golden tan on his head, and a bright tan on his chest, legs, and underparts. It is an impressive spectacle to watch the tiny dog parade around the show ring, his small delicate feet stepping sharp and his luxurious tail held high.

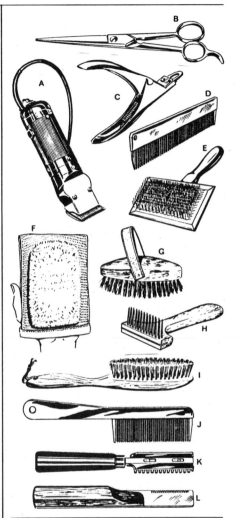

*Some of the many different grooming tools available at pet shops: A. Small animal clipper. B. 7-inch scissor. C. Nail clipper. D. Steel comb with two widths of teeth. E. Carder or slicker brush. F. Hound glove with wire center. G. Bristle brush with wire center. H. Rake. I. Bristle brush. J. Steel comb. K. Dresser. L. Stripping knife.*

# *Grooming*

The Yorkshire's coat is the breed's pride and requires constant care and protection. Grooming the Yorkshire Terrier does take a substantial amount of time, but the time will be well spent—a properly groomed Yorkie will garner compliments from all who see him.

## Brushing

Daily brushing is a task that both you and your Yorkshire Terrier will enjoy. Your pet's clean coat and healthy sheen will be a source of pride for you—and surprisingly enough, your Yorkie will seem to prance more proudly himself! Your pet will enjoy the feeling of being fresh and clean. Brushing will give him a pleasant tingling sensation and will stimulate the flow of oil in his skin. He will appreciate being free of burrs and nettles, and you will appreciate seeing the healthy hair that brushing promotes.

A thorough brushing involves three steps: (1) brush with the growth of the hair to clean the surface coat; (2) brush stiffly against the hair to clean the undercoat and massage the skin; (3) brush the hair back to its original position. These are the mechanics of brushing—a touch of loving care is the only added ingredient needed to make daily brushing fun and pleasant.

## Trimming

The ears should be scissored at the tips to where the ear begins to widen. Ears should be left quite clean. Part the hair from the base of the skull to the base of the tail, and brush down on either side with a bristle brush. Part the hair on the head at eye level from the corner of the eye to the top inside of the ear, pull upward and tie with a ribbon or barrette. Brush the fall (the long hair fringes on the face) downward.

Trim the feet with scissors following the outline of the paw, and trim the long flowing hairs only enough to even them along the bottom. The hair of the coat should touch the ground. All in all, the Yorkie should have a "rectangular" appearance.

Hair growth can be encouraged by wrapping it in wax paper or rice paper or some other porous material. This is done to develop a show coat. Section off small locks of hair, apply a small amount of baby oil, and fold each individual lock in a strip of paper, securing it with a rubber band. These wrappings

# Grooming

should not be left on for more than two or three days. Use a hair dressing or spray to complete the grooming.

Carefully tended, the coat often sweeps the ground, but some fanciers choose to keep it slightly shorter. No matter what its length, the coat must be perfectly straight and of a fine, silky texture. The keeping of a Yorkshire Terrier in "show shape" requires constant care, but breed fanciers feel that the distinctive appearance it presents makes this care worthwhile. Sweeping the ground tends to wear the ends of the coat away. Some people even put their Yorkie's hair up in curlers to prevent this from happening. When they want to show their puppy off they remove the curlers and brush out the hair— the results are magnificent.

## Bathing

When you bathe your Yorkie, which should be twice a month, choose a warm place and use several inches of warm water in a fairly deep tub. You will need a washcloth, dog soap or shampoo, and several terry-cloth towels. Wash your pet's head and ears first, using a damp washcloth and no shampoo. Then wash him from front to back and top to bottom using circular strokes and working up plenty of suds. Care should be taken to keep your pet's eyes and ears free from soap. His skin and coat should be rinsed and dried thoroughly. One word of merry admonition—your Yorkshire Terrier's natural instinct is to shake himself dry, so don't take offense if you find yourself sharing his bath! Just blame yourself for not being quick enough with the towel.

A dry shampoo, available at your local pet shop, also makes an excellent bath; you may well prefer to use such a dry shampoo on chilly days and during winter months.

# Breed Standards

A breed standard is the criterion by which the appearance (and to a certain extent, the temperament as well) of any given dog is made subject to objective measurement. Basically the standard for any breed is a definition of the perfect dog, to which all specimens of the breed are compared. The degree of excellence of the appearance of a given dog is in direct proportion to how well that dog meets the requirements for its breed.

Even the most perfect specimen of the breed falls short of the standard in some respect. It is virtually impossible for any dog to receive unanimous acclaim by everyone who compares it to the standard and to other dogs of the same breed. It is also impossible, even for a breeder or veterinarian, to tell how a puppy will shape up as an adult dog. The chances are that the puppy will inherit the qualities for which its father and mother (sire and dam) were bred, and if both parents and grandparents had good show records the puppy likely will have excellent possibilities.

Typically, a breed standard is drawn up by a national breed club (known as the parent club for that breed) and approved by the national kennel club, which is the governing body for all purebred dogs in a particular country. Any such standard is always subject to change through review by the national breed club, so it is always wise to keep up with developments in a breed by checking the publications of your national kennel club. (A list of the names and addresses of national kennel clubs for a number of English-speaking nations is included elsewhere in this book.) Although the standards of different national clubs (and competition rules and procedures) are usually very much the same, there may be variances that must be noted if you plan to become seriously involved with breeding your dog or intend to show your dog on an international basis.

So that you may get some idea of how breed standards may differ from country to country, both the American standard (as approved by the American Kennel Club) and the British standard (as approved by the Kennel Club) are presented here.

## American Standard

GENERAL APPEARANCE: That of a long-haired toy terrier whose blue and tan coat is parted on the face and from the base of the skull to the end of the tail and hangs

# Breed Standards

evenly and quite straight down each side of body. The body is neat, compact and well proportioned. The dog's high head carriage and confident manner should give the appearance of vigor and self-importance.

HEAD: Small and rather flat on top, *the skull* not too prominent or round, *the muzzle* not too long, with *the bite* neither undershot nor overshot and teeth sound. Either scissors bite or level bite is acceptable. *The nose* is black. *Eyes* are medium in size and not too prominent; dark in color and sparkling with a sharp, intelligent expression. Eye rims are dark. *Ears* are small, V-shaped, carried erect and set not too far apart.

BODY: Well proportioned and very compact. The back is rather short, the back line level, with height at shoulder the same as at the rump.

LEGS AND FEET: *Forelegs* should be straight, elbows neither in nor out. *Hind legs* straight when viewed from behind, but stifles are moderately bent when viewed from the sides. *Feet* are round with black toenails. Dewclaws, if any, are generally removed from the hind legs. Dewclaws on the forelegs may be removed.

TAIL: Docked to a medium length and carried slightly higher than the level of the back.

COAT: Quality, texture and quantity of coat are of prime importance. Hair is glossy, fine and silky in texture. Coat on the body is moderately long and perfectly straight (not wavy). It may be trimmed to floor length to give ease of movement and a neater appearance, if desired. The fall on the head is long, tied with one bow in center of head or parted in the middle and tied with two bows. Hair on muzzle is very long. Hair should be trimmed short on tips of ears and may be trimmed on feet to give them a neat appearance.

COLORS: Puppies are born black and tan and are normally darker in body color, showing an intermingling of black hair in the tan until they are matured. Color of hair on body and richness of tan on head and legs are of prime importance in *adult dogs,* to which the following color requirements apply:
*BLUE:* Is a dark steel-blue, not a silver-blue and not mingled with fawn, bronzy or black hairs.
*TAN:* All tan hair is darker at the roots than in the middle, shading to

# Breed Standards

still lighter tan at the tips. There should be no sooty or black hair intermingled with any of the tan.

COLOR ON BODY: The blue extends over the body from back of neck to root of tail. Hair on tail is a darker blue, especially at end of tail.

HEADFALL: A rich golden tan, deeper in color at sides of head, at ear roots and on the muzzle, with ears a deep rich tan. Tan color should not extend down on back of neck.

CHEST AND LEGS: A bright, rich tan, not extending above the elbow on the forelegs nor above the stifle on the hind legs.

WEIGHT: Must not exceed seven pounds.

## British Standard

GENERAL APPEARANCE: Should be that of a long-coated toy terrier, the coat hanging quite straight and evenly down each side, a parting extending from the nose to the end of the tail. The animal should be very compact and neat, the carriage being very upright and conveying an "important" air. The general outline should convey the impression of a vigorous and well-proportioned body.

HEAD AND SKULL: Head should be rather small and flat, not too prominent or round in the skull, nor too long in the muzzle, with a perfect black nose. The fall on the head to be long, of a rich golden tan, deeper in colour at the sides of the head about the ear roots, and on the muzzle where it should be very long. On no account must the tan on the head extend on to the neck, nor must there be any sooty or dark hair intermingled with any of the tan.

EYES: Medium, dark and sparkling, having a sharp intelligent expression, and placed so as to look directly forward. They should not be prominent and the edge of the eyelids should be of a dark colour.

30

# *Breed Standards*

EARS: Small V-shaped, and carried erect or semi-erect, and not far apart, covered with short hair, colour to be of a very deep rich tan.

MOUTH: Perfectly even, with teeth as sound as possible. An animal having lost any teeth through accident not to be faulted providing the jaws are even.

FOREQUARTERS: Legs quite straight, well covered with hair of a rich golden tan a few shades lighter at the ends than at the roots, not extending higher on the forelegs than the elbow.

BODY: Very compact with a good loin. Level on the top of the back.

HINDQUARTERS: Legs quite straight, well covered with hair of a rich golden tan, a few shades lighter at the ends than at the roots, not extending higher on the hind legs than the stifle.

FEET: As round as possible; the toe-nails black.

TAIL: Cut to medium length; with plenty of hair, darker blue in colour than the rest of the body, especially at the end of the tail, and carried a little higher than the level of the back.

COAT: The hair on the body moderately long and perfectly straight (not wavy), glossy like silk, and of a fine silky texture.

COLOUR: A dark steel blue (not silver blue), extending from the occiput (or back of skull) to the root of tail, and on no account mingled with fawn, bronze or dark hairs. The hair on the chest a rich bright tan. All tan hair should be darker at the roots than in the middle, shading to a still lighter tan at the tips.

WEIGHT AND SIZE: Weight up to 3.2 kg. (7 lbs).

NOTE: Male animals should have two apparently normal testicles fully descended into the scrotum.

# *Your New Puppy*

Now, assuming that you have decided that this is the right breed for you, there remain the questions of which sex and what age the puppy should be when you purchase him, the preparations to make for his arrival in your home, and the general management of the puppy once he is there.

## Sex and Age

This is no place to undertake a "battle of the sexes." Since no dog should run loose, a female, during the brief sex-vulnerable intervals of estrus twice a year, will be chaperoned whenever outdoors; or it is relatively easy to keep her safely confined or to board her with your veterinarian or at a reliable kennel. All her life she can alternate between indoor and outdoor bathroom facilities. A female usually is more gently affectionate, particularly with young children. On the other hand, a male, after he reaches an age to lift his leg, must be let or taken outside to relieve himself four times every single day, no matter what the inconvenience. He may display embarrassing interest in the sex of other dogs he encounters; leave his "calling card" on every post, tree, shrub or hydrant; and although housebroken at home, cannot always be trusted in unfamiliar private or public premises. No one can make this decision for you. "You pays your money, and takes your choice!"

As to age, two and a half to three months is young enough. By that age, a puppy is weaned and independent of his mother's care and company, day or night. He is well adapted to his diet and a convenient meal schedule. He is old enough for vaccinations against distemper and other contagious diseases (in fact, a vaccination program may have already been started for the puppy by his seller), and he is at the most responsive age to begin to understand and heed the lessons of housebreaking. A younger puppy requires frequent attention, almost foster-mothering, which cannot be delegated to children or neglected even for a few hours. A lower price at a lower age is no bargain.

## Pet versus Show Prospect

It is well to define in your own mind the purpose for which you want a dog and to convey this to the breeder. A great deal of disappointment and dissatisfaction

# *Your New Puppy*

can be avoided by a meeting of the minds between seller and buyer.

Although every well-bred, healthy member of the breed makes an ideal companion and pet, actual pet-stock is usually the least expensive of the purebred registered stock. The person who asks for a pet pays a pet-geared price for the animal. Pet stock is least expensive because these dogs are deemed unsuitable for breeding or exhibition in comparison to the standard of perfection for the breed. Generally, only skilled breeders and judges can point out the structural differences between pet- and show-quality dogs.

If you are planning to show your dog, make this clear to the breeder and he will aid you in selecting the best possible specimen of the breed. A show-quality dog may be more expensive than one meant for a pet, but it will be able to stand up to show-ring competition.

## Where to Buy Your Puppy

Once you have decided on the particular breed that you want for your pet, your task is to find that one special dog from among several outlets. Buying a well-bred, healthy dog is your foremost concern. By doing a little research in the various dog magazines and newspapers, you can locate the names and addresses of breeders and kennels in your area that are known for breeding quality animals. Your national dog club will also furnish you with addresses of people to contact who are knowledgeable about your chosen breed.

Your local pet shop, although necessarily restricted from carrying all breeds in stock, may sometimes be able to supply quality puppies on demand. Due to the exorbitant amount of space and time needed to properly rear puppies, pet shops generally prefer to assist owners by supplying all the tools and equipment needed in the raising and training of the puppies. The pet shop proprietor, if unable to obtain a dog for you, can often refer you to a reputable kennel with which he has done business before.

## Selection

When you do pick out a puppy as a pet, don't be hasty; the longer you study puppies, the better you will understand them. Make it your transcendent concern to select only one that radiates good health and spirit and is lively on his feet, whose eyes are bright, whose coat shines, and who comes forward eagerly to make and to cultivate your acquaintance. Don't fall for any shy little darling that wants to retreat to his bed or his box, or plays coy behind other puppies or people, or hides his head under your arm or jacket appealing to your protective instinct. *Pick the puppy who forthrightly picks you! The feeling of attraction should be mutual!*

## Documents

Now, a little paper work is in order. When you purchase a purebred puppy, you should receive a transfer of ownership, registration material, and other "papers" (a list of the immunization shots, if any, the puppy may have been given; a note on whether or not the puppy has been wormed; a diet and feeding schedule to which the puppy is accustomed) and you are welcomed as a fellow owner to a long, pleasant association with a most lovable pet, and more (news)paper work.

## General Preparation

You have chosen to own a particular puppy. You have chosen it very carefully over all other breeds and all other puppies. So before you ever get that puppy home, you will have prepared for its arrival by reading everything you can get your hands on having to do with the management of dogs and puppies. True, you will run into many conflicting opinions, but at least you will not be starting "blind." Read, study, digest. Talk over your plans with your veterinarian, other "dog people," and the seller of your puppy.

When you get your puppy, you will find that your reading and study are far from finished. You've just scratched the surface in your plan to provide the greatest possible comfort and health for your puppy; and, by the same token, you do want to assure yourself of the greatest possible enjoyment of this wonderful creature. You must be ready for the puppy mentally as well as in the physical requirements.

## Transportation

If you take the puppy home by car, protect him from drafts, particularly in cold weather. Wrapped in a towel and carried in the arms or lap of a passenger, the puppy usually will make the trip without mishap. If the pup starts to

# *Your New Puppy*

drool and to squirm, stop the car for a few minutes. Have newspapers handy in case of car-sickness. A covered carton lined with newspapers provides protection for puppy and car, if you are driving alone. Avoid excitement and unnecessary handling of the puppy on arrival. A puppy is a very small "package" to be making complete change of surroundings and company, and he needs frequent rest and refreshment to renew his vitality.

## The First Day and Night

When your puppy arrives in your home, put him down on the floor and don't pick him up again, except when it is absolutely necessary. He is a dog, a real dog, and must not be lugged around like a rag doll. Handle him as little as possible, and permit no one to pick him up and baby him. To repeat, *put your puppy on the floor or the ground and let him stay there except when it may be necessary to do otherwise.*

Quite possibly your puppy will be afraid for a while in his new surroundings, without his mother and littermates. Comfort him and reassure him, but don't console him. Don't give him the "oh-you-poor-ittsy-bitsy-puppy" treatment. Be calm, friendly, and reassuring. Encourage him to walk around and sniff over his new home. If it's dark, put on the lights. Let him roam for a few minutes while you and everybody else concerned sit quietly or go about your routine business. Let the puppy come back to you.

Playmates may cause an immediate problem if the new puppy is to be greeted by children or other pets. If not, you can skip this subject. The natural affinity between puppies and children calls for some supervision until a live-and-let-live relationship is established. This applies particularly to a Christmas puppy, when there is more excitement than usual and more chance for a puppy to swallow something upsetting. It is a better plan to welcome the puppy several days before or after the holiday week. Like a baby, your puppy needs much rest and should not be over-handled. Once a child realizes that a puppy has "feelings" similar to his own, and can readily be hurt or injured, the opportunities for play and responsibilities provide exercise and training for both.

For his first night with you, he should be put where he is to sleep every night—say the kitchen, since its floor can usually be easily

35

# Your New Puppy

cleaned. Let him explore the kitchen to his heart's content; close doors to confine him there. Prepare his food and feed him lightly the first night. Give him a pan with some water in it—not a lot, since most puppies will try to drink the whole pan dry. Give him an old coat or a shirt to lie on. Since a coat or shirt will be strong in human scent, he will pick it out to lie on, thus furthering his feeling of security in the room where he has just been fed.

## Housebreaking Helps

Now, sooner or later—mostly sooner—your new puppy is going to "puddle" on the floor. First take a newspaper and lay it on the puddle until the urine is soaked up onto the paper. *Save this paper.* Now take a cloth with soap and water, wipe up the floor and dry it well. Then take the wet paper and place it on a fairly large square of newspapers in a convenient corner. When cleaning up, always keep a piece of wet paper on top of the others. Every time he wants to "squat," he will seek out this spot and use the papers. (This routine is rarely necessary for more than three days.) Now leave your puppy for the night. Quite probably he will cry and howl a bit; some are more stubborn than others on this matter. But let him stay alone for the night. This may seem harsh treatment, but it is the best procedure in the long run. Just let him cry; he will weary of it sooner or later.

## Beat Him to the Draw

Puppies, like human infants, wake up at the crack of dawn. So, bright and early, your first job is to take him outdoors for a "business trip." Try to keep him out until he has relieved himself. Then give him his first meal of the day, after which you take him out again. Puppies usually want to relieve themselves first thing in the morning, last thing at night, after each feeding, and after each nap. To cut down on "mistakes," take him out often for the first few days, until he learns what he is going out for—and keep him near his newspapers. Caution: Do not force him to rely too much on the newspapers or he will get to the point where he will stay out for hours without doing anything and then rush to the papers when he at last is brought indoors.

Housebreaking is a simple thing if done properly. Just cooperate with the inevitable! Anticipate his need

# *Your New Puppy*

before he does. And for the first few mistakes, say nothing to him—especially the first 24 hours. Then, when he misbehaves, point to the error and quietly but firmly say "No" or "Fooey!" Make it decisive. He must know he has done wrong, but he must *not* be scared to death. And under no circumstance must he be slapped, yelled at, or stamped at. Just a brisk "Fooey" or "No." Work things in such a way that he doesn't get a chance to misbehave.

## Collar and Leash Training

Now as to general management, immediately put on him a small leather collar and have a leash to go with it. He probably won't notice the collar at all; but if he does, and seems to fight it, let him fight it and pay no attention. He'll get used to it quickly. Leave it on all the time. Whenever he goes outside, snap a leash onto the collar. City or country, always take your dog out with collar and leash. This is his first taste of discipline. And discipline is not punishment—it is training!

All training is done on the leash. He may buck and plunge a bit at first, finding himself unable to run around at will. Hold the leash

firmly, but let it "give" a lot for the first few days. Do not start him off with the chain collar. Such a collar is ideal later, but it is painful and even dangerous on a young puppy. Gradually teach him to walk quietly on the leash, always on your left side. Hold the leash in such a way to prevent him from running ahead of you or crossing your path. By all means, start his leash- and-collar work as soon as you get him. Don't start his formal training until he is five or six months old, or maybe a little older, depending on the dog himself. Meanwhile, he is learning what "No" means, and he is learning to come when called. Always speak his name first, followed by the command "Come." And make it a command, but slap your knees to encourage him at first. Study your training book now, even though you won't start regular training for months.

## Riding in the Car

Start your puppy off right in the car. He will probably have to be boosted in the first few times. Let him sit on the floor. Take him only on short trips for awhile. If the excitement or motion of riding makes him sick, he will begin to

# *Your New Puppy*

drool heavily. When you see this, stop the car and take him out. Let him walk around on the leash a bit—say five or ten minutes. Then put him back in the car and start off again. For several weeks, go for short trips only and make the trips frequent. The younger the puppy, usually the sooner he learns to like driving and the less he is concerned with it.

Take your puppy everywhere—streets, stores—everywhere. Do it in easy stages, but get him accustomed to all sorts of strange sights, sounds, and smells. Thus, when he is mature, he will go anywhere with perfect poise.

Encourage him, too, to stand quietly and be patted by strangers. Be careful that he doesn't learn to dislike children, as sometimes happens with dogs of all breeds, because of rough handling on the part of the children. Let one or two children take him for a walk on his leash once in a while. Let them feed him some special treat as they take him out.

## Introducing New Situations

In general, either lead your puppy or encourage him to take the initiative in all new situations. Don't ever "push" him into them. You will get nowhere and may end up spoiling the dog.

With you and your family, observe the same procedures. Let the dog make the move. Encourage him to sit or lie quietly with the family. Let the dog develop into a sensible, normal dog. Don't fuss with him constantly.

Do not misunderstand the instruction not to make a fuss over the puppy. This does not mean you should bring up your dog in a harsh, strict manner. A dog has a limitless reservoir of love and affection and devotion for those he knows and loves. Sure, play with him. Sure, roughhouse with him, but don't make an addlepated ninny out of him by constantly fooling or talking with him. If there is anything worse than a spoiled child, it's a spoiled dog. Both are a pain in the neck to all concerned. So bring up your puppy to be a friendly, well-mannered, happy, healthy dog. If he doesn't "get around," how can he know how to act under all circumstances? So take him around. Start his training early.

## To Spay or Not to Spay

To spay a female dog (past tense,

# *Your New Puppy*

*spayed)* is to remove both ovaries from the dog surgically, thus rendering it impossible for the dog ever to have puppies or periods of "heat," or "season." And make no mistake about it, this is major surgery to be performed only by a graduate, licensed veterinarian. However, in his hands, the practice of spaying is quite generally used and is considered a routine operation. The risk involved is almost zero, assuming that the dog is of correct age and is in excellent health and condition.

Needless to say, there is considerable difference of opinion on spaying. "Spay and spoil your female" is the contention of those who are opposed, although just how the female is "spoiled" is not readily apparent. The opponents will tell you that the spayed female becomes sluggish, dull, has no pep or joy in life, gets enormously fat, and wants only to eat and sleep. It is further alleged that the spayed female is rendered stupid and unable to learn anything.

Now, among old-timers in the dog game, there is a very strong conviction that the female is a far better companion and housedog than the male, and the best housedog and companion is a spayed female. These experienced

dog keepers have never seen a fat, stupid spayed female; and they firmly believe that spaying in no way affects the dog's personality or characteristic joy in living. Granted, there is a tendency to get fat, but this situation is easily regulated by proper feeding.

To anyone not interested in breeding dogs but who wants a fine companion and housedog, the spayed female has no superior. Always beautiful anyway, she is keen, smart, and lively.

## Special Care for the Brood Bitch

If your female is to be used as a breeding animal, there are certain topics to be covered in the management of the female during her periods of heat.

The female usually comes in heat for the first time between the ages of seven and 12 months. And allowing for some variations in individual dogs, the female will come in heat roughly twice a year, once in the spring and once in the fall, or thereabouts.

The onset of the heat period is marked by a slight discharge of dark red blood from the vulva, or external genital organ, of the female.

39

# *Your New Puppy*

With this discharge, odorless to humans, comes a gradual swelling and enlargement of the vulva, along with an increased flow of blood, until the ninth or tenth day, at which time the vulva is quite enlarged and the flow has begun to be pinkish or amber colored. The discharge gradually pales out and decreases during the third week. But while the heat period is usually considered to be three weeks, it is much safer to count it a month in duration.

If you live in the city, the heat period will cause you little if any inconvenience, since, in the city, dogs are more apt to be leashed or more carefully controlled than dogs in the suburbs and country. But the safe rule, to guard against accidental breeding, is to keep your female always on a lead throughout the entire heat period. As for the droplets of discharge around the house, they are odorless and may easily be removed by wiping with a damp cloth.

In the country or suburbs, you may have somewhat of a problem. Again, take your female outside only on a leash and keep her close beside you. If possible, walk her a little way from the house to relieve herself, keeping a sharp lookout for visiting males. Some males are extremely fast operators; and unless you are very careful, especially from the seventh or eighth day on, you may have an unwanted breeding before you know it. In this instance, once such a breeding has begun, there is absolutely nothing you can do about it. Attempted separation of the two animals will result in serious injury to both. However, should you have such bad luck, immediately take your female to your veterinarian. Sometimes he can prevent a litter of mutts.

Indoors, continue your caution. Along about the eleventh or twelfth day, your female may sneak outside if not watched, and she is sure to run into a group of waiting males. Keep her under lock and key for a full month!

b

# *Feeding*

Now let's talk about feeding your dog, a subject so simple that it's amazing there is so much nonsense and misunderstanding about it. Is it expensive to feed a dog? No, it is not! You can feed your dog economically and keep him in perfect shape the year round, or you can feed him expensively. He'll thrive either way, and let's see why this is true.

First of all, remember a dog is a dog. Dogs do not have a high degree of selectivity in their food, and unless you spoil them with great variety (and possibly turn them into poor, "picky" eaters) they will eat almost anything that they become accustomed to. Many dogs flatly refuse to eat nice, fresh beef. They pick around it and eat everything else. But meat—bah! Why? They aren't accustomed to it! They are hounds. They'd eat rabbit fast enough, but they refuse beef because they aren't used to it.

## Variety Not Necessary

A good general rule of thumb is forget all about human preferences and don't give a thought to variety. Choose the right diet for your dog and feed it to him day after day, year after year, winter and summer. But what is the right diet?

Hundreds of thousands of dollars have been spent in canine nutrition research. The results are pretty conclusive, so you needn't go into a lot of experimenting with trials of this and that every other week. Research has proven just what your dog needs to eat and to keep healthy.

## Dog Food

There are almost as many right diets as there are dog experts, but the basic diet most often recommended is one that consists of a dry food, either meal or kibble form. There are several of these of excellent quality, manufactured by reliable concerns, research tested, and nationally advertised. They are inexpensive, highly satisfactory, and easily available in stores everywhere in containers of five to fifty pounds. Larger amounts cost less per pound, usually.

# Feeding

If you have a choice of brands, it is usually safer to choose the better-known one; but even so, carefully read the analysis on the package. Do not choose any food in which the protein level is less than 25 percent, and be sure that this protein comes from both animal *and* vegetable sources. The good dog foods have meat meal, fish meal, liver, and such, plus protein from alfalfa and soybeans, as well as some dried-milk product. Note the vitamin content carefully. See that they are all there in good proportions; and be especially certain that the food contains properly high levels of vitamins A and D, two of the most perishable and important ones. Note the B-complex level, but don't worry about carbohydrate and mineral levels. These substances are plentiful and cheap and not likely to be lacking in a good brand.

The advice given for how to choose a dry food also applies to moist or canned types of dog foods, if you decide to feed one of these.

Having chosen a really good food, feed it to your dog as the manufacturer directs. And once you've started, stick to it. Never change if you can possibly help it. A switch from one meal or kibble-type food can usually be made without too much upset; however, a change will almost invariably give you (and the dog) some trouble.

## Fat Important; Meat Optional

While the better dog foods are complete in themselves in every respect, there is one item to add to the food, and that is *fat*—any kind of melted animal fat. It can be lard, bacon, or ham fat or from beef, lamb, pork, or poultry. A grown dog should have at least a tablespoon or two of melted fat added to one feeding a day. If you feed your dog morning and night, give him half of the fat in each feeding.

The addition of meat to this basic ration is optional. There is a sufficient amount of everything your dog needs already in the food, but you may add any meat you wish, say, a half to a quarter of a pound. In adding meat, the glandular meats are best, such as kidneys, pork liver, and veal or beef heart. They are all cheap to buy and are far higher sources of protein than the usual muscle meat humans insist on. Cook these meats slightly or feed them raw. Liver and kidney should be cooked a little and fed sparingly since they are laxative to some dogs. Heart is ideal, raw or cooked. Or you can feed beef, lamb, ocean fish well cooked, and pork.

# Feeding

## When Supplements Are Needed

Now what about supplements of various kinds, mineral and vitamin, or the various oils? They are all okay to add to your dog's food. However, if you are feeding your dog a correct diet, and this is easy to do, no supplements are necessary unless your dog has been improperly fed, has been sick, or is having puppies. Vitamins and minerals are naturally present in all foods; and to ensure against any loss through processing, they are added in concentrated form to the dog food you use. Except on the advice of your veterinarian, extra and added amounts of vitamins can prove harmful to your dog! The same risk goes with minerals.

## Feeding Schedule

When and how much food to give your dog? As to when (except in the instance of puppies which will be taken up later), suit yourself. You may feed two meals per day or the same amount in one single feeding, either morning or night. As to how to prepare the food and how much to give, it is generally best to follow the directions on the food package. Your own dog may want a little more or a little less.

Fresh, cool water should always be available to your dog. This is important to good health throughout his lifetime.

## All Dogs Need to Chew

Puppies and young dogs need something with resistance to chew on while their teeth and jaws are developing—for cutting the puppy teeth, to induce growth of the permanent teeth under the puppy teeth, to assist in getting rid of the puppy teeth at the proper time, to help the permanent teeth through the gums, to ensure normal jaw development, and to settle the permanent teeth solidly in the jaws.

The adult dog's desire to chew stems from the instinct for tooth cleaning, gum massage, and jaw exercise—plus the need for an outlet for periodic doggie tensions.

This is why dogs, especially puppies and young dogs, will often destroy property worth hundreds of dollars when their chewing instinct is not diverted from their owner's possessions. And this is why you should provide your dog with something to chew—something that

# *Feeding*

has the necessary functional qualities, is desirable from the dog's viewpoint, and is safe for your dog.

It is very important that dogs not be permitted to chew on anything they can break or on any indigestible thing from which they can bite sizeable chunks. Sharp pieces, such as from a bone which can be broken by a dog, may pierce the intestinal wall and kill. Indigestible things which can be bitten off in chunks, such as from shoes or rubber or plastic toys, may cause an intestinal stoppage (if not regurgitated) and bring painful death, unless surgery is promptly performed.

Strong natural bones, such as 4- to 8-inch lengths of round shin bone from mature beef—either the kind you can get from a butcher or one of the variety available commercially in pet stores—may serve your dog's teething needs if his mouth is large enough to handle them effectively. You may be tempted to give your puppy a smaller bone and he may not be able to break it when you do, but puppies grow rapidly and the power of their jaws constantly increases until maturity. This means that a growing dog may break one of the smaller bones at any time, swallow the pieces, and die painfully before you realize what is wrong.

All hard natural bones are highly abrasive. If your dog is an avid chewer, natural bones may wear away his teeth prematurely; hence, they then should be taken away from your dog when the teething purposes have been served. The badly worn, and usually painful, teeth of many mature dogs can be traced to excessive chewing on natural bones.

Contrary to popular belief, knuckle bones which can be chewed up and swallowed by the dog provide little, if any, useable calcium or other nutriment. They do, however, disturb the digestion of most dogs and cause them to vomit the nourishing food they need.

Dried rawhide products of various types, shapes, sizes, and prices are available on the market and have become quite popular. However, they don't serve the primary chewing functions very well; they are a bit messy when wet from mouthing, and most dogs chew them up rather rapidly—but they have been considered safe for dogs until recently. Now, more and more incidents of death, and near death, by strangulation have been reported to be the result of partially swallowed chunks of rawhide swelling in the throat. More

# *Feeding*

recently, some veterinarians have been attributing cases of acute constipation to large pieces of incompletely digested rawhide in the intestine.

The nylon bones, especially those with natural meat and bone fractions added, are probably the most complete, safe, and economical answer to the chewing need. Dogs cannot break them or bite off sizeable chunks; hence, they are

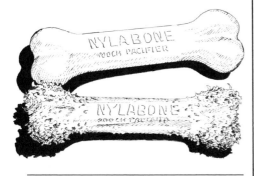

*The upper Nylabone has not yet been chewed; the lower Nylabone shows normal signs of wear.*

completely safe—and being longer lasting than other things offered for the purpose, they are economical.

Hard chewing raises little bristle-like projections on the surface of the nylon bones—to provide effective interim tooth cleaning and vigorous gum massage, much in the same way your toothbrush does it for you. The little projections are raked off and swallowed in the form of thin shavings, but the chemistry of the nylon is such that they break down in the stomach fluids and pass through without effect.

The toughness of the nylon provides the strong chewing resistance needed for important jaw exercise and effectively aids teething functions, but there is no tooth wear because nylon is non-abrasive. Being inert, nylon does not support the growth of microorganisms; and it can be washed in soap and water or it can be sterilized by boiling or in an autoclave.

Nylabone® is highly recommended by veterinarians as a safe, healthy nylon bone that can't splinter or chip. Nylabone® is frizzled by the dog's chewing action, creating a toothbrush-like surface that cleanses the teeth and massages the gums. Nylabone® and Nylaball® the only chew products made of flavor-impregnated solid nylon, are available in your local pet shop.

Nothing, however, substitutes for periodic professional attention to your dog's teeth and gums, not any more than your toothbrush can do that for you. Have your dog's teeth cleaned by your veterinarian at least once a year (twice a year is better) and he will be healthier, happier, and far more pleasant to live with.

# Training

You owe proper training to your dog. The right and privilege of being trained is his birthright; and whether your dog is going to be a handsome, well-mannered housedog and companion, a show dog, or whatever possible use he may be put to, the basic training is always the same—all must start with basic obedience, or what might be called "manners training."

Your dog must come instantly when called and obey the "Sit" or "Down" command just as fast; he must walk quietly at "Heel," whether on or off the lead. He must be mannerly and polite wherever he goes; he must be polite to strangers on the street and in stores. He must be orderly in the presence of other dogs. He must not bark at children on roller skates, motorcycles, or domestic animals. And he must be restrained from chasing cats. It is not a dog's inalienable right to chase cats, and he must be reprimanded for it.

## Professional Training

How do you go about this training? Well, it's a very simple procedure, pretty well standardized by now. First, if you can afford the extra expense, you may send your dog to a professional trainer, where in 30 to 60 days he will learn how to be a "good dog." If you enlist the services of a good professional trainer, follow his advice about when to come to see the dog. No, he won't forget you, but too-frequent visits at the wrong time may slow down his training progress. And using a "pro" trainer means you will have to go for some training, too, after the trainer feels your dog is ready to go home. You will have to learn how your dog works, just what to expect of him and how to use what the dog has learned after he is home.

## Obedience Training Class

Another way to train your dog (many experienced dog people think this is the best) is to join an obedience-training class right in your own community. There is such a group in nearly every community nowadays. Here you will be working with a group of people who are also just starting out. You will actually be training your own dog, since all work is done under the direction of a head trainer who will make suggestions to you and also tell you when and how to correct your dog's errors. Then, too, working with such a group, your dog will learn to get along with other dogs. And, what is more important, he will learn to do exactly what he is told to do, no matter how much confusion there is around him or how great the temptation to go his own way.

Write to your national kennel club for the location of a training club or class in your locality. Sign up. Go to it regularly—every session! Go early and leave late! Both you and your dog will benefit tremendously.

## Train Him By The Book

The third way of training your dog is by the book. Yes, you can do it this way and do a good job of it too. If you can read and if you're smarter than the dog, you'll do a good job. But in using the book method, select a book, buy it, study it carefully; then study it some more, until the procedures are almost second nature to you. *Then* start your training. But stay with the book and its advice and exercises. Don't start in and then make up a few rules of your own. If you don't follow the book, you'll get into jams you can't get out of by yourself. If after a few hours of short training sessions your dog is

still not working as he should, get back to the book for a study session, because it's *your* fault, not the dog's! The procedures of dog training have been so well systematized that it must be your fault, since literally thousands of fine dogs have been trained by the book.

After your dog is "letter perfect" under all conditions, then, if you wish, go on to advanced training and trick work.

Your dog will love his obedience training, and you'll burst with pride at the finished product! Your dog will enjoy life even more, and you'll enjoy your dog more. And remember—you *owe* good training to your dog!

*There are a number of good books that give detailed training information.*

# Showing

A show dog is a comparatively rare thing. He is one out of several litters of puppies. He happens to be born with a degree of physical perfection that closely approximates the standard by which the breed is judged in the show ring. Such a dog should, at maturity, be able to win or approach his championship in good, fast company at the larger shows. Upon finishing his championship, he is apt to be highly desirable as a breeding animal. As a proven stud, he will automatically command a high price for service.

Showing dogs is a lot of fun—yes, but it is a highly competitive sport. Though all the experts were once beginners, the odds are against a novice. You will be showing against experienced handlers, both pro and amateur, people who have devoted a lifetime to breeding, picking the right ones, and then showing those dogs through to their championships. Moreover, the most perfect dog ever born has faults, and in your hands the faults will be far more evident than with the experienced handler who knows how to minimize his dog's faults. There are but a few points on the sad side of the picture.

The experienced handler, however, was not born knowing the ropes. He learned—*and so can you!* You can if you will put in the same time, study, and keen observation that he did. But it will take time!

## Key to Success

First, search for a truly fine show-prospect puppy. Take the puppy home, raise him by the book, and, as carefully as you know how, give him every chance to mature into the dog hoped for. Some dog experts recommend keeping a show-prospect puppy out of big shows, even Puppy Classes, until he is mature. When he is approaching maturity, break him in at match shows (more on these later); after this experience for the dog and you, then go gunning for the big wins at the big shows.

# *Showing*

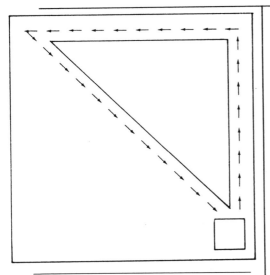

*Although there are different patterns to follow when gaiting your dog, this is the one most frequently used.*

Next step: read the standard by which the breed is judged. Study it until you know it by heart. Having done this—and while your puppy is at home (where he should be) growing into a fine normal, healthy dog—go to every dog show you can possibly reach. Sit at the ringside and watch the judging. Keep your ears and eyes open. Do your own judging, holding each of those dogs against the standard, which you now know by heart.

In your evaluations, don't start off looking for faults. Look for the virtues—the best qualities. How does a given dog shape up against the standard? Having looked for and

noted the virtues, then note the faults and see what prevents a given dog from standing correctly or moving well. Weigh these faults against the virtues, since, ideally, every feature of the dog should contribute to the harmonious whole.

## "Ringside Judging"

It's a good practice to make notes on each dog, always holding the dog against the standard. In "ringside judging," forget your personal preference for this or that feature. What does the standard say about it? Watch carefully as the judge places the dogs in a given class. It is difficult from the ringside always to see why number one was placed over the second dog. Try to follow the judge's reasoning. Later try to talk with the judge after he is finished (not every judge will have the time or inclination for this). Ask him questions as to why he placed certain dogs and not others. Listen while the judge explains his placings.

When you're not at the ringside, talk with the fanciers and breeders. Don't be afraid to ask opinions or say that you don't know. You have a lot of listening to do, and it will help you a great deal and speed up

# *Showing*

your personal progress if you are a good listener.

## Join the Clubs

You will find it worthwhile to join the national kennel club, which is the governing body for all purebred dogs in a particular country, and to subscribe to its magazine, if one is published. From this national kennel club, you can learn the location of the national breed club (known as the "parent club" for that breed), which you also should join. Being a member of these clubs will afford you the opportunity to get to know other people who share your interests and concerns, to learn more about your breed, and to find out when and where match shows and point shows will be held.

For information regarding sanctioned shows in most English-speaking areas, write to one of the kennel clubs listed below:

American Kennel Club
51 Madison Avenue
New York, NY 10010
USA

Australian Kennel Club
Royal Show Grounds
Ascot Vale, Victoria
Australia

British Kennel Club
1 Clarges Street
London 41Y 8AB
England

Canadian Kennel Club
2150 Bloor Street West
Toronto, Ontario M6S 4V7
Canada

Irish Kennel Club
23 Earlsfort Terrace
Dublin 2
Ireland

## Prepare for the Show

The first thing you must do to prepare for a show is to find out the dates and rules of the show you intend to attend. Write to the national kennel club and get a copy of their show dates and rules (and rules for obedience competition or field trials or whatever type of competition you are interested in).

You also must teach your dog and yourself some basics of dog showing. You must learn to "stack" your dog, and your dog must learn to stay in this show stance whenever required to do so. Your dog must learn to accept being examined by a stranger (in other words, the judge at the show). You will have to learn how to gait your dog, and your dog must learn how to move properly at your side.

## Enter Match Shows

Match shows differ from regular shows only in that no championship points are given. These shows are especially designed to launch young dogs (and young handlers) on a show career.

With the ring deportment you have watched at big shows firmly in mind and practice, enter your dog in as many match shows as you can. When in the ring, you have two jobs. One is to see to it that your dog is always being seen to best advantage. The other job is to keep your eye on the judge to see what he may want you to do next. Watch only the judge and your dog. Be quick and be alert; do exactly as the judge directs. Don't speak to him except to answer his questions. If he does something you don't like, don't say so. And don't irritate the judge (and everybody else) by constantly talking and fussing with your dog.

In moving about the ring, remember to keep clear of dogs beside you or in front of you. Many dog fanciers feel that you should *not* show your dog in a regular point show until he is at least close to maturity and after both you and he have had time to perfect ring manners and poise in the match shows.

## Point Shows

Point shows are for purebred dogs registered with the club that is sanctioning the show. Each dog is entered in the show class which is appropriate for his age, sex, and previous show record. The show classes usually include Puppy, Novice, Bred-by-Exhibitor, American-bred, and Open; and there may also be a Veterans Class and Brace and Team Classes, among others.

There also may be a Junior Showmanship Class, a competition for youngsters. Young people between the ages of 10 and 16, inclusively, compete to see who best handles their dog, rather than to see which dog is best, as is done in the other classes.

For a complete discussion of show dogs, dog shows, and showing a dog, read *Successful Dog Show Exhibiting* by Anna Katherine Nicholas (T.F.H. Publications, Inc.).

# Breeding

So you have a female dog and you want to breed her for a litter of puppies. Wonderful idea—very simple—lots of fun—make a lot of money. Well, it *is* a wonderful idea, but stop right there. It's not very simple—and you won't make a lot of money. Having a litter of puppies to bring up is

*The external skeletal parts of a dog: 1. Cranium. 2. Cervical vertebra. 3. Thoracic vertebra. 4. Rib. 5. Lumber vertebra. 6. Ilium. 7. Femur. 8. Fibula. 9. Tibia. 10. Tarsus. 11. Metatarsus. 12. Phalanges. 13. Phalanges. 14. Ulna. 15. Radius. 16. Humerus. 17. Scapula.*

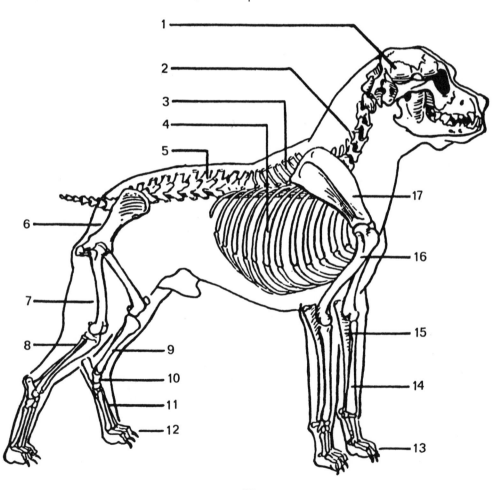

# *Breeding*

hard, painstaking, thoughtful work; and only a few people regard such work as fun.

## Breed Better Dogs

Bear in mind this very important point: Being a dog breeder is not just breeding dear Tillie to that darned good-looking male down the street. Would that it were that simple! Such a breeding will undoubtedly produce puppies. But that is not all you want. When you breed your female, it is only after the most careful planning—with every effort being made to be sure that the resulting puppies will be even better than the parent dogs (that they will come even closer to the standard than the parent animals) and that all the puppies will have good homes. Any fool can breed a litter of puppies; but only a careful, thoughtful, intelligent person can breed a litter of better puppies of your breed of dog. That must be your goal in breeding!

You can become a good novice breeder if you truly love the breed and are seriously concerned with the past, present, and future of the breed. You will breed your female only according to established scientific principles. Your personal

sentiments have no place in the careful planning that goes on before you actually breed your female. The science of mammalian genetics is not a precise science like, say, mathematics. And the extensive reading you will do on the science (or art) of breeding dogs before you start to choose a stud will give you some idea of the variable factors you will be dealing with. It is a vast subject; but with the few brief pointers given here and additional reading and study, you can at least start on the right track.

## Plan It on Paper

The principles of animal breeding are the same, whether the subjects be beef cattle, poultry, or dogs. To quote a cattle breeder, every breeding is first made "on paper" and later in the barnyard. In other words, first the blood strains of the animals are considered as to what goes well with what, so far as recorded ancestry is concerned. Having worked this out, the two animals to be mated must be studied and compared. If one does not excel where the other is lacking, at least in most points, then the paper planning must start over again and different animals be considered.

# Breeding

With your own dog, there are several "musts" that are really axioms. First, breed only the best to the best. Two inferior animals will produce nothing but inferior animals, as surely as night follows day. To breed an inferior dog to another inferior one is a crime against the breed. So start by breeding the best to the best. And here again, an accurate knowledge of the standard is essential to know just what is best.

### "Compensation" Breeding

No perfect dog has yet been whelped. Your female may be a winning show dog. She may be a champion. But she does have faults. In breeding her to a fine male, you must consider "compensation" breeding. She must compensate for his shortcomings and he for hers. For example, your female may be ideal in most respects but have faulty feet. So the male you choose, however ideal in other respects, *must* have ideal feet, as had his sire and dam too. In this way you may overcome the foot faults in your female's puppies.

This same principle applies to the correction of faults in any section of either male or female. But, you say, my dog has a pedigree as long as your arm. Must be good! Sad but true, a pedigree will not necessarily produce good puppies. A pedigree is no more—and no less—than your dog's recorded ancestry. Yes, you must know what dogs are in your dog's pedigree, but the most important point is, Were they good dogs? What were their faults and virtues? And to what degree did these dogs transmit these faults and virtues?

### Breeding Methods

Now you may have heard that "like begets like." This is true and it is also false! Likes can beget likes only when both parent animals have the same likeness through generations of both family lines. The only way known to "fix" virtues and to eliminate faults is to mate two dogs of fairly close relationship bloodwise, two dogs which come from generations of likes and are family-related in their likeness. In this way you may ensure a higher and regular percentage of puppies which can be expected to mature into adults free at least from major faults under the standard. The likes must have the same genetic inheritance.

Through this "family" breeding, or line-breeding, correct type is set

# Care of Mother and Family

and maintained. If both family lines are sound to begin with, family breeding and even close inbreeding (mating closely related dogs such as father and daughter) will merely improve the strain—but only in skilled hands. "Outcrossing" is mating dogs of completely different bloodlines with no, or only a few, common ancestors; it is used when undesirable traits begin to haunt closer breeding or when the breeder wants to bring in a specific trait or feature. The finest dogs today are the result of just such breeding methods. Study, expert advice, and experience will enable you, a novice, to follow these principles. So in your planning, forget the old nonsense about idiots and two-headed monsters coming from closely related parents.

Then, too, in your planning and reading, remember that intangible virtues, as well as physical ones, are without doubt inherited, as are faults in those intangibles. For example, in breeding bird dogs, where "nose sense" is of greatest importance, this factor can to a degree be fixed for future generations of puppies when the ancestors on both sides have the virtue of "nose sense." Just so, other characteristics of disposition or temperament can be fixed.

Let us assume that you have selected the right stud dog for your female and that she has been bred. In some 58 to 63 days, you will be presented with a nice litter of puppies. But there are a number of things to be gone over and prepared for in advance of the whelping date.

Before your female was bred, she was, of course, checked by your veterinarian and found to be in good condition and free from worms of any sort. She was in good weight but not fat. Once your female has been bred, you should keep your veterinarian informed of your female's progress; and when the whelping is imminent, your vet should be informed so that he can be on call in case any problems arise.

There's an old saying, "A litter should be fed from the day the bitch is bred," and there is a world of truth in it. So from the day your female is bred right up to the time the puppies are fully weaned, the mother's food is of the greatest importance. Puppies develop very rapidly in their 58 to 63 days of gestation, and their demands on the mother's system for nourishment are great. In effect, you are feeding your female and one to six or more other dogs, all at the same time.

# Care of Mother and Family

*The color captions for pages 57-64 can be found on page 16.*

## Additions to Regular Diet

For the first 21 days, your female will need but few additions to her regular diet. Feed her as usual, except for the addition of a small amount of "pot " or cottage cheese. This cheese, made from sour milk, is an ideal, natural source of added protein, calcium, and phosphorus—all essential to the proper growth of the unborn litter. Commercial vitamin-mineral supplements are unnecessary if the mother is fed the proper selection of natural foods.

Most commercial supplements are absolutely loaded with mineral calcium. You will usually find that the bulk of the contents is just plain calcium, a cheap and plentiful substance. Some dog experts believe, however, that calcium from an animal source like cheese is far more readily assimilated, and it is much cheaper besides. At any rate, do not use a commercial supplement without consulting your veterinarian and telling him the diet your dog is already getting.

## Increase Food Intake

Along about the fifth week, the litter will begin to show a little, and now is the time to start an increase in food intake, not so much in bulk as in nutritive value. The protein content of your female's regular diet should be increased by the addition of milk products (cottage cheese, for example) meat (cooked pork liver, raw beef or veal heart, or some other meat high in protein), and eggs (either the raw yolk alone or, if the white is used, the egg should be cooked). Meanwhile, high-calorie foods should be decreased. The meat, cut into small pieces or ground, can be added to the basic ration. Mineral and vitamin supplements and cod-liver oil or additional fat also can be given to the female at this point, if your veterinarian so recommends.

## Feed Several Times A Day

By now, your female is but a few weeks away from her whelping date, and the growing puppies are compressing her internal organs to an uncomfortable degree. She will have to relieve herself with greater frequency now. The stomach, too, is being compressed, so try reducing

BEST OF
WINNERS
GREATER OCALA
DOG CLUB

PHOTO BY *Graham*

# Care of Mother and Family

the basic ration slightly and at the same time increasing the meats, eggs, and milk products. Feed several small meals per day in order to get in the proper, stepped-up quantity of food without causing the increased pressure of a single large meal. The bitch should be fed generously, but she should not be allowed to become overweight.

## Regular Exercise Important

A great deal of advice has been given by experts on keeping the female quiet from the day she is bred all through the pregnancy. Such quiet, however, is not natural and it cannot be enforced. Naturally, the female should not be permitted to go in for fence jumping; but she will be as active as ever during the first few weeks and gradually she will, of her own accord, slow down appropriately, since no one knows quite as much about having puppies as the dog herself—up to a point. But see to it that your female has plenty of gentle exercise all along. She'll let you know when she wants to slow down.

*The color captions for pages 57-64 can be found on page 16.*

Treat her normally, and don't let her be the victim of all the sentimentality that humans with impending families are heir to.

## Whelping Imminent

About the morning of the 58th day or shortly thereafter, your female, who now looks like an outsize beer barrel, will suddenly refuse her food. She may drink water, however. If you have been observant as things progressed, your hand, if not your eye, will tell you that the litter has dropped. The female now has a saggy abdomen, and this is the tip-off that whelping will occur soon, usually well within the next 24 hours. As the actual whelping hour approaches, the mother will become increasingly restless. She will seek out dark places like closets. She will scratch at the floor and wad up rugs as if making a bed. She is pretty miserable right now, so be gently sympathetic with her but *not maudlin!*

Get her to stay in the whelping box you have had prepared for several days. The floor of the box should be covered with an old blanket or towel so that she will feel comfortable there. When the whelping starts, replace the bedding

# Care of Mother and Family

with newspapers; these can be replaced as they get scratched up or soiled.

The whelping box should be located in a warm, not hot, place free from drafts. The area should also be fairly quiet. You may, if you wish, confine her to the box by hitching her there with a leash to a hook three or four feet off the floor so she won't get twisted up in it. But when actual whelping starts, take off both leash and collar. Then, get yourself a chair and prepare for an all-night vigil. Somehow puppies always seem to be born at night, and the process is good for 12 to 14 hours usually.

## Labor Begins

Stay with her when she starts to whelp, you and one other person she knows well and who is an experienced breeder. No audience, please! A supply of warm water, old turkish towels, and plenty of wiping rags are in order at this point.

When labor commences, the female usually assumes a squatting position, although some prefer to lie down. The first puppy won't look much like a puppy to you when it is fully expelled from the female. It will be wrapped in a dark, membranous sac, which the mother will tear open with her teeth, exposing one small, noisy pup—very wet. Let the mother lick the puppy off and help to dry it. She will also bite off the navel cord. This may make the puppy squeal, but don't worry, mama is not trying to eat her pup. The mother may eat a few of the sacs; this is normal. When she is through cleaning the puppy off, pick up the puppy and gently but firmly give it a good rubbing with a turkish towel. Do this in full sight of the mother and close enough so that she will not leave her whelping box.

When the puppy is good and dry and "squawking" a bit, place it near the mother or in a shallow paper box close to the mother so she can see it but will not step on it when she becomes restless with labor for the second puppy. If the room temperature is lower than 70 degrees, place a hot-water bottle wrapped in a towel near the puppies. Be sure to keep the water changed and warm so the puppies aren't lying on a cold water bottle. Constant warmth is essential.

Most dogs are easy whelpers, so you need not anticipate any trouble. Just stay with the mother, more as an observer than anything else. The experienced breeder who is keeping you company, or your vet, should handle any problems that arise.

66

# Care of Mother and Family

## Post-natal Care

When you are reasonably certain that the mother has finished whelping, have your veterinarian administer the proper amount of obstetrical pituitrin. This drug will induce labor again, thus helping to expel any retained afterbirth or dead puppy.

Inspect your puppies carefully. Rarely will any deformities be found; but if there should be any, make a firm decision to have your veterinarian destroy the puppy or puppies showing deformities.

During and after whelping, the female is very much dehydrated, so at frequent intervals she should be offered lukewarm milk or meat soup, slightly thickened with well-soaked regular ration. She will relish liquids and soft foods for about 24 hours, after which she will go back to her regular diet. But be sure she has a constant supply of fresh water available. Feed her and keep her water container outside the whelping box.

After all of the puppies have been born, the mother might like to go outside for a walk. Allow her this exercise. She probably won't want to be away from her puppies more than a minute or two.

The puppies will be blind for about two weeks, with the eyes gradually opening up at that time.

The little pups will be quite active and crawl about over a large area. Be sure that all of the puppies are getting enough to eat. If the mother sits or stands, instead of lying still to nurse, the probable cause is scratching from the puppies nails. You can remedy this by clipping them, as you do hers.

## Weaning Time

Puppies can usually be completely weaned at six weeks of age, although you can start to feed them at three weeks. They will find it easier to lap semi-solid food. At four weeks they should be given four meals a day, and soon they will do without their mother entirely. Start them on mixed dog food, or leave it with them in a dish for self-feeding. Don't leave water with them all the time; at this age everything is to play with and they will use it as a wading pool. They can drink all they need if it is offered several times a day, after meals.

As the puppies grow up, the mother will go into the box only to nurse them, first sitting up and then standing. The periods of time between the mother's visits to the box will gradually lengthen, until it is no longer necessary for her to nurse the pups.

# Health and Disease

First, don't be frightened by the number of health problems that a dog might have over the course of his life-time. The majority of dogs never have any of them. Don't become a dog-hypochondriac. All dogs have days when they feel lazy and want to lie around doing nothing. For the few problems that you might be concerned about, remember that your veterinarian is your dog's best friend. When you first get your puppy, select a veterinarian whom you have faith in. He will get to know your dog and will be glad to have you consult him for advice. A dog needs little medical care, but that little is essential to his good health and well-being. He needs a proper diet given at regular hours; clean, roomy housing; daily exercise; companionship and love; frequent grooming; and regular check-ups by your veterinarian.

## Using a Thermometer and Giving Medicines

Almost every serious ailment shows itself by an increase in the dog's body temperature. If your dog acts lifeless, looks dull-eyed, and gives the impression of illness,

*The proper way to give a pill or tablet.*

check his temperature by using a rectal thermometer made of either plastic or glass. Hold the dog securely, insert the thermometer (which you have lubricated with petroleum jelly), and take a reading. The average normal temperature for your dog will be 101.5°F. Excitement may raise the temperature slightly; but any rise of

*The proper way to give liquid medication.*

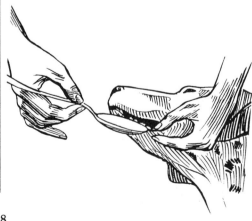

# Health and Disease

more than a few points is cause for alarm, and your vet should be consulted.

Giving medicines to your dog is not really difficult. In order to administer a liquid medication, do not open the dog's mouth. Instead, form a pocket by pulling out the lower lip at the corner of the mouth; pour the medicine in with a spoon; hold the head only very slightly upward. (If the head is held too high, the medicine may enter the windpipe instead of the passage to the stomach, thus choking the dog.) With agitated animals, medicine can still be given by this method, even though the dog's mouth is held shut with a tape or a muzzle.

In order to administer a pill or tablet, raise your dog's head slightly and open his mouth. (Using one hand, grasp the cheeks of the dog, and then press inward. The pressure of the lips pushed against the teeth will keep the mouth open). With the other hand, place the pill or tablet far back on the middle of the tongue. Quickly remove your hand from the dog's cheeks; hold the dog's mouth closed (but not too tightly), and gently massage his throat. You can tell the medicine has been swallowed when the tip of the dog's tongue shows between his front teeth.

## A Vaccination Schedule

*Prevention* is the key word for many dog diseases, and the best prevention is a series of vaccinations administered by your veterinarian. Such contagious diseases as distemper, hepatitis, parainfluenza, leptospirosis, rabies, and canine parvovirus can be virtually eliminated by strictly following a vaccination schedule.

*Distemper* is probably the most virulent of all dog diseases. Young dogs are most susceptible to it, although it may affect dogs of all ages. The dog will lose his appetite, seem depressed, feel chilled, and run a fever. Often he will have a watery discharge from his eyes and nose. Unless treated promptly, the disease goes into advanced stages with infections of the lungs, intestines, and nervous system; and dogs that recover may be left with some impairment such as paralysis, convulsions, a twitch, or some other defect, usually spastic in nature. The best protection against this is very early inoculation with a series of permanent shots and a booster shot each year thereafter.

*Hepatitis* is a viral disease spread by contact. The initial symptoms of drowsiness, vomiting, great thirst, loss of appetite, and a high temperature closely resemble those

# Health and Disease

of distemper. These symptoms are often accompanied by swellings of the head, neck, and abdomen. The disease strikes quickly; death may occur in just a few hours. Protection is afforded by injection with a vaccine.

*Parainfluenza* is commonly called "kennel cough." Its main symptom is coughing; and since it is highly contagious, it can sweep through an entire kennel in just a short period of time. A vaccination is a dog's best protection against this respiratory disease.

*Leptospirosis* is caused by bacteria that live in stagnant or slow-moving water. It is carried by rats and mice, and infection is begun by the dog licking substances contaminated by the urine or feces of infected animals. The symptoms are diarrhea and a yellowish-brownish discoloration of the jaws, tongue, and teeth, caused by an inflammation of the kidneys. This disease can be cured if caught in time, but it is best to ward it off with a vaccine which your veterinarian can administer.

*Rabies* is an acute disease of the dog's central nervous system. It is spread by infectious saliva transmitted by the bite of an infected animal. Rabies is generally manifested in one or the other of two groups of symptoms, and the symptoms usually appear within five days. The first is "furious rabies," in which the dog exhibits changes in his personality. The dog becomes hypersensitive and runs at and bites everything in sight. Eventually, the animal's lower jaw becomes paralyzed and hangs down; he walks with a stagger and saliva drips from his mouth. The second syndrome is referred to as "dumb rabies" and is characterized by the dog's walking in a bearlike manner, head down. The lower jaw is paralyzed, and the dog is unable to bite. Outwardly, it may seem as though he has a bone caught in his throat.

Even if your pet should be bitten by a rabid dog or other animal, he probably can be saved if you get him to the veterinarian in time for a series of injections. However, after the symptoms have appeared, no cure is possible. Remember that an annual rabies inoculation is almost certain protection against rabies. If you suspect that your dog or some other animal has rabies, notify your local health department. A rabid animal is a danger to all who come near him.

*Canine parvovirus* is a highly contagious viral disease that attacks the intestinal tract, white blood cells, and less frequently the heart muscle. It is believed to spread through dog-to-dog contact (the

# Health and Disease

specific source of infection being the fecal matter of infected dogs), but it can also be transmitted from place to place on the hair and feet of infected dogs and by contact with contaminated cages, shoes, and the like. It is particularly hard to overcome because it is capable of existing in the environment for many months under varying conditions, unless strong disinfectants are used.

The symptoms are vomiting, fever, diarrhea (often blood-streaked), depression, loss of appetite, and dehydration. Death may occur in only two days. Puppies are hardest hit, with the virus being fatal to 75 percent of the puppies that contact it. Older dogs fare better; the disease is fatal to only two to three percent of those afflicted.

The best preventive measure for parvovirus is vaccination administered by your veterinarian. Precautionary measures individual pet owners can take include disinfecting the kennel and other areas where the dog is housed. One part sodium hypochlorite solution (household bleach) to 30 parts of water will do the job efficiently. Keep the dog from coming into contact with the fecal matter of other dogs when walking or exercising your pet.

## Internal Parasites

There are four common internal parasites that may infect your dog. These are roundworms, hookworms, whipworms, and tapeworms. The first three can be diagnosed by laboratory examination; the presence of tapeworms is determined by seeing segments in the stool or attached to the hair around the tail. Do not under any circumstances attempt to worm your dog without the advice of your veterinarian. After first determining what type of worm or worms are present, he will advise you of the best method of treatment.

A dog or puppy in good physical condition is less susceptible to worm infestation than a weak dog. Proper sanitation and a nutritious diet help in preventing worms. One of the best preventive measures is to always have clean, dry bedding for

*Adult whipworms are between two and three inches long, and the body of each worm is no thicker than a heavy sewing needle.*

# Health and Disease

your dog. This will diminish the possibility of reinfection due to flea or tick bites.

Heartworm infestation in dogs is passed by mosquitoes and can be a life-threatening problem. Dogs with the disease tire easily, have difficulty breathing, cough, and may lose weight despite a hearty appetite. If caught in the early stages, the disease can be effectively treated; however, the administration of daily preventive medicine throughout the spring, summer, and fall months is strongly advised. Your veterinarian must first take a blood sample from your dog to test for the presence of the disease. If the dog is heartworm-free, pills or liquid medicine can be prescribed that will protect against any infestation.

*Above: Red mange mite.*

*Below: The common dog flea.*

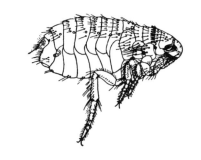

A female dog tick that is gorged with blood.

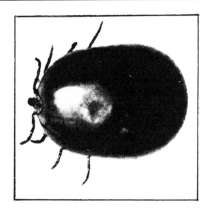

*Below: The under side of a sarcoptic mange mite.*

# Health and Disease

## External Parasites

Fleas and ticks are the two most common external parasites that can trouble a dog. Along with the general discomfort and irritation that they bring to a dog, these parasites can infest him with worms and disease. The flea is a carrier of tapeworm and may act as an intermediate host for heartworm. The tick can cause dermatitis and anemia, and it may also be a carrier of Rocky Mountain spotted fever and canine babesiasis, a blood infection. If your dog becomes infested with fleas, he should be treated with a medicated dip bath or some other medication recommended by your vet. Ticks should be removed with great care;

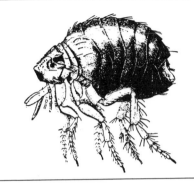

*A sticktight flea.*

you must be certain that the head of the tick is not left in the dog—this could be a source of infection.

Two types of mange, sarcoptic and follicular, are also caused by parasites. The former is by far the more common and results in an intense irritation, causing violent scratching. Close examination will reveal small red spots which become filled with pus. This is a highly

---

*A female tick.*

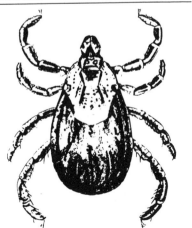

---

*A male tick.*

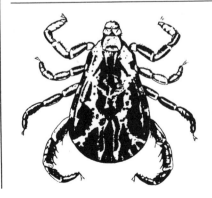

# Health and Disease

contagious condition, and any dog showing signs of the disease should be isolated. Consult your veterinarian for the proper treatment procedures. Follicular mange is very much harder to cure; but fortunately, it is much rarer and less contagious. This disease will manifest itself as bare patches appearing in the skin, which becomes thickened and leathery. A complete cure from this condition is only rarely effected.

## Other Health Problems

*Hip dysplasia* is an often crippling condition more prevalent in large

*A dislocation of the upper leg bone. Dislocations should be immediately attended to by your vet.*

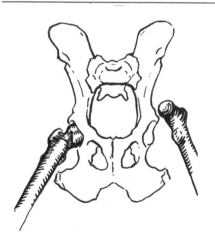

breeds than in small, but it has occurred in almost every breed. The cause is not known absolutely, though it is believed to be hereditary, and as yet there is no known cure. The condition exists in varying degrees of severity. In general, hip dysplasia can be described as a poor fit between the two bones of the hip joint and is caused by a malformation of one or the other. The condition causes stiffness in the hindlegs, considerable pain in the more severe cases, and difficulty of movement. It generally manifests itself in puppyhood and can be noticed by the time the young dog is two months old. If hip dysplasia is suspected, the dog should be x-rayed; and if afflicted, it should not be used for breeding. When the pain is severe and continual, euthanasia is occasionally recommended, though medication is available to control the pain and allow the dog to move with more ease.

*Coughs, colds, bronchitis, and pneumonia* are respiratory diseases that may affect the dog. Being subjected to cold or a draft after a bath, sleeping near an air conditioner or in the path of a fan, or resting near a radiator can cause respiratory ailments. The symptoms are similar to those in humans;

however, the germs of these diseases are different and do not affect both dogs and humans, so they cannot be infected by each other. Treatment is much the same as for a child with the same type of illness. Keep the dog warm, quiet, and well fed. Your veterinarian has antibiotics and other remedies to help the dog recover.

*Eczema* is a disease that occurs most often in the summer months and affects the dog down the back, especially just above the root of the tail. It should not be confused with mange, as it is not caused by a parasite. One of the principle causes of eczema is improper nutrition, which makes the dog susceptible to disease. Hot, humid weather promotes the growth of bacteria, which can invade a susceptible dog and thereby cause skin irritation and lesions. It is imperative that the dog gets relief from the itching that is symptomatic of the disease, as self-mutilation by scratching will only help to spread the inflammation. Antibiotics may be necessary if a bacterial infection is, indeed, present.

*Moist eczema,* commonly referred to as "hot spots," is a rapidly appearing skin disease that produces a moist infection. Spots appear very suddenly and may spread rapidly in a few hours, infecting several parts of the body. These lesions are generally bacterially infected and are extremely itchy, which will cause the dog to scratch frantically and further damage the afflicted areas. Vomiting, fever, and an enlargement of the lymph nodes may occur. The infected areas must be clipped to the skin and thoroughly cleaned. Your veterinarian will prescribe an anti-inflammatory drug and antibiotics, as well as a soothing emollient to relieve itching.

The *eyes,* because of their sensitivity, are prone to injury and infection. Dogs that spend a great deal of time outdoors in heavily wooded areas may return from an exercise excursion with watery eyes, the result of brambles and high weeds scratching them. The eyes may also be irritated by dirt and other foreign matter. Should your dog's eyes appear red and watery, a mild solution can be mixed at home for a soothing washing. Your veterinarian will be able to tell you what percentage of boric acid, salt, or other medicinal compound to mix with water. You must monitor your dog's eyes after such a solution is administered; if the irritation persists, or if there is a significant discharge, immediate veterinary attention is warranted.

Your dog's *ears,* like his eyes, are extremely sensitive and can also be

# Health and Disease

prone to infection, should wax and/or dirt be allowed to build up. Ear irritants may be present in the form of mites, soap or water, or foreign particles which the dog has come into contact with while romping through a wooded area. If your dog's ears are bothering him, you will know it—he will scratch his ears and shake his head, and the ears will have a foul-smelling dark secretion. This pasty secretion usually signals the onset of *otorrhea*, or ear canker, and at this stage proper veterinary care is essential if the dog's hearing is not to be permanently impaired. In the advanced stages of ear canker, tissue builds up within the ear, and the ear canal becomes blocked off, thus diminishing the hearing abilities of that ear. If this is to be prevented, you should wash your dog's ears, as they require it, with a very dilute solution of hydrogen peroxide and water, or an antibacterial ointment, as your vet suggests. In any case,

*An ear mite.*

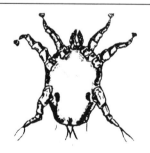

the ears, because of their delicacy, are to be washed gently, with a soft cloth or cotton.

Your pet's *teeth* can be maintained by his regular use of a chew product such as Nylabone® or Nylaball,® which serves to clean the teeth of tartar accumulation and to massage and stimulate the gums. Tartar accumulates on the teeth of dogs, particularly at the gum line, more rapidly than on the teeth of humans; and these accumulations, if not removed, bring irritation, infection and, ultimately, destruction of the teeth at the roots. With puppies, a chew product helps to relieve the discomfort of the teething stage and, of course, prevents the pup's chewing of your furniture and slippers! A periodic inspection of your dog's mouth will alert you to any problem he might have which would require a trip to the veterinarian's office. Any signs of tooth or gum sensitivity, redness, or swelling, signal the need for professional treatment.

A dog's *nails* should not be allowed to become overlong. If you live in a city and walk your dog regularly on pavement, chances are that his nails are kept trimmed from the "wear and tear" they receive from the sidewalks. However, if your dog gets all of his exercise in your yard, or if his nails simply grow rather quickly, it will occasionally be necessary for you to clip his nails. It is best for you to have your veterinarian show you the proper way to perform the nail clipping. Special care must always be taken to avoid cutting too far and reaching the "quick." If you cut into the quick of the nail, it will bleed, so it is easy to see why an expert must show you the proper procedure. A nail clipper designed especially for dogs can be purchased at any pet shop.

## Emergency First Aid

If you fear that your dog has swallowed *poison*, immediately get him to the veterinarian's. Try to locate the source of poisoning; if he has swallowed, for example, a cleaning fluid kept in your house, check the bottle label to see if inducing the dog to vomit is necessary. Inducing the dog to vomit can be very harmful, depending upon the type of poison swallowed. Amateur diagnosis is very dangerous.

*Accidents,* unfortunately, do happen, so it is best to be prepared. If your dog gets hit by a car or has a bad fall, keep him absolutely quiet, move him as little as possible, and get veterinary treatment as soon as possible. It is unwise to give any stimulants such as brandy or other alcoholic liquids when there is visible external hemorrhage or the possibility of internal hemorrhaging.

*Minor cuts and wounds* will be licked by your dog, but you should treat such injuries as you would your own. Wash out the dirt and apply an antiseptic.

*Severe cuts and wounds* should be bandaged as tightly as possible to stop the bleeding. A wad of cotton may serve as a pressure bandage, which will ordinarily stop the flow of blood. Gauze wrapped around the cotton will hold it in place. Usually applying such pressure to a wound will sufficiently stop the blood flow; however, for severe bleeding, such as when an artery is cut, a tourniquet may be necessary. Apply a tourniquet between the injury and the heart if the bleeding is severe. To tighten the tourniquet, push a pencil through the bandage and twist it. Take your dog to a veterinarian immediately, since a tourniquet should not be left in place any longer than fifteen minutes.

*Minor burns or scalds* can be treated by clipping hair away from the affected area and then applying a paste of bicarbonate of soda and water. Apply it thickly to the burned area and try to keep the dog

# Care of the Oldster

from licking it off.

*Serious burns* require the immediate attention of your veterinarian, as shock quickly follows such a burn. The dog should be kept quiet, wrapped in a blanket; and if he still shows signs of being chilled, use a hot-water bottle. Clean the burn gently, removing any foreign matter such as bits of lint, hair, grass, or dirt; and apply cold compresses. Act as quickly as possible. Prevent exposure to air by covering with gauze, cotton, and a loose bandage. To prevent the dog from interfering with the dressing, muzzle him and have someone stay with him until veterinary treatment is at hand.

*Stings* from wasps and bees are a hazard for the many dogs that enjoy trying to catch these insects. A sting frequently follows a successful catch, and it often occurs inside the mouth, which can be very serious. The best remedy is to get him to a veterinarian as soon as possible, but there are some precautionary measures to follow in the meantime. If the dog has been lucky enough to be stung only on the outside of the face, try to extricate the stinger; then swab the point of entry with a solution of bicarbonate of soda. In the case of a wasp sting, use vinegar or some other acidic food.

B arring accident or disease, your dog is apt to enjoy a life of 12 to 14 years. However, beginning roughly with the eighth year, there will be a gradual slowing down. And with this there are many problems of maintaining reasonably good health and comfort for all concerned.

While there is little or nothing that can be done in the instance of failing sight and hearing, proper management of the dog can minimize these losses. Fairly close and carefully supervised confinement are necessary in both cases. A blind dog, otherwise perfectly healthy and happy, can continue to be happy if he is always on a leash outdoors and guided so that he does not bump into things. Indoors, he will do well enough on his own. Dogs that are sightless seem to move around the house by their own radar system. They learn where objects are located; but once they do learn the pattern, care must be taken not to leave a piece of furniture out of its usual place.

Deafness again requires considerable confinement, especially in regard to motor traffic and similar hazards; but deafness curtails the dog's activities much less than blindness. It is not necessary to send any dog to the Great Beyond because it is blind or deaf—if it is otherwise healthy and seems to enjoy life.

Teeth in the aging dog should be watched carefully, not only for the pain they may cause the dog but also because they may poison the system without any local infection or pain. So watch carefully, especially when an old dog is eating. Any departure from his usual manner should make the teeth suspect at once. Have your veterinarian check the teeth frequently.

## His System Slows Down

As the dog ages and slows down in his physical activity, so his whole system slows down. With the change, physical functions are in some instances slowed and in others accelerated—in effect, at least.

For example, constipation may occur; and bowel movements may become difficult, infrequent, or even painful. Chronic constipation is a problem for your veterinarian to deal with; but unless it is chronic, it is easily dealt with by adding a little extra melted fat to the regular food. Do not increase roughage or administer physics unless so directed by your veterinarian. If the added

fat in the food doesn't seem to be the answer to occasional constipation, give your dog a half or a full teaspoon of mineral oil two or three times a week. Otherwise, call your veterinarian.

On either side of the rectal opening just below the base of the tail are located the two anal glands. Occasionally these glands do not function properly and may cause the dog great discomfort if not cleaned out. This is a job for your veterinarian, until after he has shown you how to do it.

## Watch His Weight

In feeding the aging dog, try to keep his weight down. He may want just as much to eat as ever, but with

*An easy way to weigh your dog is to hold the dog while you stand on a scale, and then subtract your weight from the total.*

# Care of the Oldster

decreased activity he will tend to put on weight. This weight will tend to slow down all other bodily functions and place an added strain on the heart. So feed the same diet as usual, but watch the weight.

Age, with its relaxing of the muscles, frequently makes an otherwise clean dog begin to misbehave in the house, particularly so far as urination is concerned. There is little that can be done about it, if your veterinarian finds there is no infection present, except to give your dog more frequent chances to urinate and move his bowels. It's just a little bit more work on your part to keep your old friend more comfortable and a "good" dog.

Let your dog exercise as much as he wants to without encouraging him in any violent play. If he is especially sluggish, take him for a walk on a leash in the early morning or late evening. Avoid exercise for him during the heat of the day. And in cold weather or rain, try a sweater on him when he goes out. It's not "sissy" to put a coat on an old dog. You and your veterinarian, working closely together, can give your dog added life and comfort. So consult your veterinarian often.

Occasionally in an old dog there is a problem of unpleasant smell, both bodily and orally. If this situation is acute, it is all but unbearable to have the dog around. But the situation can be corrected or at least alleviated with frequent and rather heavy dosing of chlorophyll. A good rubdown with one of the dry-shampoo products is also helpful.

## When the End Comes

People who have dogs are sooner or later faced with the tragedy of losing them. It's tough business losing a dog, no matter how many you may have at one time. And one dog never takes the place of another—so don't expect it to. When you lose your dog, get another as quickly as you can. It does help a lot.

Keep your dog alive as long as he is happy and comfortable. Do everything you reasonably can to keep him that way. But when the sad time comes that he is sick, always uncomfortable, or in some pain, it is your obligation then to have him put away. It is a tough ordeal to go through, but you owe it to your old friend to allow him to go to sleep. And, literally, that's just what he does. Your veterinarian knows what to do. And your good old dog, without pain, fright, bad taste, or bad smells, will just drift to sleep.